THE *devil* GOES TO WORK TOO

Yvette,

Thanks for your support! May everyday you know the peace and joy of God.

Carl o B Jay

THE *devil* GOES TO WORK TOO

CARLOS B. TAYLOR

authorHOUSE®

AuthorHouse™
1663 Liberty Drive
Bloomington, IN 47403
www.authorhouse.com
Phone: 1 (800) 839-8640

© 2015 Carlos B. Taylor. All rights reserved.

No part of this book may be reproduced, stored in a retrieval system, or transmitted by any means without the written permission of the author.

Published by AuthorHouse   08/28/2015

ISBN: 978-1-5049-2151-0 (sc)
ISBN: 978-1-5049-2152-7 (e)

Print information available on the last page.

Any people depicted in stock imagery provided by Thinkstock are models, and such images are being used for illustrative purposes only. Certain stock imagery © Thinkstock.

This book is printed on acid-free paper.

Because of the dynamic nature of the Internet, any web addresses or links contained in this book may have changed since publication and may no longer be valid. The views expressed in this work are solely those of the author and do not necessarily reflect the views of the publisher, and the publisher hereby disclaims any responsibility for them.

Scripture quotations marked NIV are taken from the Holy Bible, New International Version®. NIV®. Copyright © 1973, 1978, 1984 by International Bible Society. Used by permission of Zondervan. All rights reserved. [Biblica]

Scripture quotations marked KJV are from the Holy Bible, King James Version (Authorized Version). First published in 1611. Quoted from the KJV Classic Reference Bible, Copyright © 1983 by The Zondervan Corporation.

Contents

Foreword vii
Dedication ix
Prologue xi

On The Third Day 1
Day Two 9
Day Three 12
Recognition 15
And The Blessings Keep Coming 19
God Is At Work! 21
Retrospection 29
Stretching Out On Faith (A Yearning On The Inside) 32
Change Is Inevitable 36
Things Change. Deal With It 45
A Place For Me 49
Sunnyside-Up 52
Purpose And Provision 62
In Transition 65
Follow The Leader 70
Dump The Applecart 73
Be Still And Know 79
Carpooling With The Devil 86
The $800,000 Meeting 90
You Are Not The Boss Of Me 95

All In A Day's Work… 102
Fair Is Fair?? 105
Sometimes You Got To Beat A Dead Horse 108
Escape To Paradise 113
You Got To Be Kidding Me 116
Give Praise 122
Thank You Lord 123
It Is What It Is… 126

References 131
About the Author 133

Foreword

As an accomplished leader who cherishes God, Family, and Faith, Carlos Taylor shares how God has been present and instrumental at every step in his career. His words of experience and Mom's Messages will be beneficial for anyone who wants to grow, achieve, and live a healthy work-life balance!
Donny Zamora
President
MEDS –

Inspiring, relevant, and practical... The Devil Goes to Work Too is a road map for those determined to be successful at work and in life in spite of any challenges thrown before them. Carlos Taylor is a true testament that belief, perseverance, a positive outlook are the keys to a prolific life and one where failure is not an option.
Christopher Cullom
Hospital Administrator

Dedication

To God for showing me all things are possible, for without him the thoughts that occupy the pages of this book would not be. To my parents who provided a fertile ground for me to plant the memories of my life. To my family, friends, co-workers and mentors for the stories and memories we shared through the years. This book serves as my testimony of GOD's unmerited favor and his mercies granted towards me. I hope readers will be constantly reminded that God is truly omniscient, omnipotent and omnipresent.

Prologue

6Be strong and courageous. Do not be afraid or terrified because of them, for the Lord your God goes with you; he will never leave you nor forsake you." (Deuteronomy 31:6, NIV)

The first chapter of "The Devil Goes to Work Too" is actually the last chapter of the book. My desire is the reader reads this chapter at the beginning of the book and then again when they have completed the other chapters. My thought, the end is not the end for me but points to a new and greater beginning, Christ demonstrates this through his crucifixion and resurrection.

While the miracles and wonders Jesus performed before being crucified were all amazing displays of his power and position in the household of faith, his arising from the grave with all powers in heaven and earth was a message to the world that he lives and reigns supremely forever. Having knowledge of his life and resurrection gives purpose to my existence and ignites a fire on the inside, a fire that drives me to offer up my testimony of God's true and ever presence in my life.

Many times I have faced moments I thought I would not rebound from. I paused to wonder if all my good days were gone. On the contrary, God in all of his wisdom brought me to the end of each road to allow me to revive and refocus so he could prepare my heart and mind for the new work he would begin in me. A work greater than any work he has entrusted me to do before.

As I embark on my journey to find truth, embark on my journey to find myself I move forward knowing the path of Faith I have chosen is as sure as the promises of God. Each day, each new experience, evolving into the person God's sees me to be, uniquely evolving.

On The Third Day

> **6**being confident of this, that he who began a good work in you will carry it on to completion until the day of Christ Jesus. (Phillipians1:6, NIV)

One Monday afternoon I received an unexpected visit from my boss and the Director of Human Resources. They were there to notify me that they were terminating my employment with the organization. My thoughts immediately went to the cross, I was being crucified and convicted based on trumped up charges. As those that persecuted Christ thought the crucifixion was the end for him, my accusers were there to declare this would be my end. This experience has been the most significantly spiritual and life changing moment in my career. Within three days I was persecuted, declared dead, and resurrected for God's glory.

The day started out like a typical Monday, I was scurrying around the office at 7AM preparing for my weekly 10AM meeting with my boss. My Monday ritual consisted of me putting the finishing touches on my reports, querying the supervisors and managers about accounts or why our numbers were down in a particular area. Fortunately I didn't have many questions to ask of the staff today because we were off to a great start for the month. The projections showed we were going to end the month with our highest monthly collections of the year. Before I knew it the time for me to walk over to my boss' office was upon me. I arrived there a couple of minutes early. My boss, Mr. Do-Little-Or-Nothing was sitting behind his desk. I greeted him and he greeted me as he headed over to the table where I was sitting. I began to update him on the numerous projects my three departments were working on. After I completed my project update, I started to go over the numbers on the dashboard. My boss listened intently as I discussed the stats. He would interject periodically to ask for clarification or make a comment. Once I completed the review my boss said good work. I responded "Thanks".

After the business part of the meeting was completed, I asked Mr. Do-Little-or-Nothing had he done any running lately. He stated he had done some running but not as much as he would have liked. I told him I had run eleven miles over the weekend in preparation for a half-marathon. Mr. Do-Little-or-Nothing gave me advice on how to prepare before the race and shared some tips on how to avoid cramps and dehydration during the race. I ended the conversation and headed back to my office.

I worked a couple of hours after returning to the office then made my daily lunch run to Chick-fil-A. I brought my usual, a grilled chicken sandwich and a fruit cup and headed back to work. As I pulled into the office parking lot, I noticed Throw-Stones-N-Hide-Her-Hands standing in front of the building talking on her cell-phone. She looked in my direction

The Devil Goes To Work Too

I acknowledged her by waving my hand and entered the building. Approximately an hour later, the visitors arrived. The HR representative and my boss walked into my office and took a seat. The HR representative lead the conversation, my boss barely spoke and deliberately avoided looking in my direction. The HR representative spoke in a very stern voice. He told me I was being terminated for having a conversation with several employees. I asked him who were the employees I had spoken with, he offered no response. I asked him what was told to him by the employees, again no there was response to the question. I asked if I could tell him my side of the story, he said he didn't need to hear it. Realizing I was not going to get any answers regarding the matter I was being terminated for, I directed my questions towards my financial situation. The HR representative informed me I wouldn't receive severance and would not be paid for the vacation time I accumulated during my two years and nine months on the job. He told me the only benefit I would have for the next month would be health insurance. I asked several other questions about unemployment benefits and other financial matters, he declined to answer those questions.

After the formalities of the conversation were out of the way, my boss exited the room and returned with a box for me to put my belongings in. The box was my cross and the allegations thrown at me were nails and a crown of thorns. As if the moment wasn't dramatic enough, I had to compose myself to leave my office and face all of my employees who were at their desks and in the hallway. I was being put on display for the world to witness my demise. Mr. Do-Little-Or-Nothing opened the door to my office. He and the HR guy walked out ahead of me. I took one long deep breath before I exited the office for the last time. I exited the building, walked about fifteen feet to my car. Mr. Do-Little-Or-Nothing, the HR guy and I placed my belongings in the car. My boss told me he was confident I would rebound and learn from this experience. I am not sure if his comments were sincere or not, at that moment I didn't find them to be encouraging. His words were like offering a drowning man a glass of water. I offered a final good bye to my former boss, shook his hand, got in the car and drove away.

I must say for a person who was just relieved from a six figure job I was calm and composed. I would even say I felt great resolve as I drove away. Unfortunately, someone speed dialed Satan to tell him I was in a vulnerable position; Satan being the scoundrel that he is showed up in true form filling my head with doubts and fears. All hope was gone. I began to think of how my termination would reflect on my reputation, what the staff I left behind would think, how was I going to tell my family, and if I could rebound from this unfortunate experience. Listening to gospel music usually perk up my spirit so I turned on the gospel station attempting to

The Devil Goes To Work Too

drown out the devil's voice; He wasn't deterred a bit, he spoke louder. I decided I would drive to the gym, a good workout normally helps clear my mind. The drive to the gym takes about twenty minutes; today it seemed to take hours. I finally reached my destination, parked the car and decided to call my friend Tell-it-like-it-is to tell him what happened. "Hey man." He replied, "What's up Evolving?" "Man I got fired today." "For real, what happened?" I told him what happened. "That's really ********** man, those are some evil bastards." Now in addition to feeling depressed about my current situation. I am mad. I echo my friend's anger by adding negative comments of my own. I think Tell-it-like-it-is detected his comments were only making a bad situation worse so he began telling me that my firing was a blessing. "How do you think this is a good thing?" I replied. He responded, "Man, you losing that job is God's way of removing Your fence, he is about to increase your territory and add a blessing to your life." Tell-it-like-it-is words of encouragement drew my thoughts back to a positive place. "Thanks for the positive words man, I appreciate you. I just arrived at the gym, I will call you later." "Alright Evolving, I will talk to you later."

At the gym, I couldn't not get myself together, I felt like everyone knew I lost my job. I walked around aimlessly for twenty minutes until I finally decided I would get started. I warmed up 10 minutes on the Stairmaster, stretched a bit and before I knew it my mind was wondering again. I looked down onto the first floor and saw a work out buddy entering the weight room. I did not want to talk about my termination so I decided to end my work-out and head home. I arrived home around 6PM, unloaded some of my work belongings from the car. After unloading the car, I checked the mailbox, walked in the house and plopped down into my favorite chair. I sat there staring at the ceiling for a few minutes. I didn't see it at the time but I was the guest of honor at one of the biggest pity parties you have ever seen. I was a mess. In the midst of my internal struggle, I noticed I had a missed text. The text was from my friend, Focused. It read: "How's it going"? I replied, "It's going I got fired today." My response was in part due to my paranoia. I thought somehow he already knew about my firing, but asked the question in an attempt to get me to talk about it. He texted back, "Do you want to talk?" I called him; "Hey man." He replied, "Man, I am sorry about that, I can't believe it." I spent some of the conversation talking about what happened but most of the conversation was about next steps. At the end of the conversation, Focused said "I will meet you at the library tomorrow we will look for jobs and work on our resumes." I replied, "See you tomorrow I will be there at 9:30." "Cool, see you then" Focus replied.

After the phone call, I decided it was time for me to share the news with my family. Deciding who to call first is a major deal for me. I thought I would tell my dad first because he is not an emotional person, but I knew if

I tell him he would tell my mom and she would be upset that I didn't tell her first. My mom is very spiritual, wise and I know she will offer me some good advice. On the other hand, she is also very emotional and those people fired her baby. I want her advice, but I don't want to listen to her go off on a tangent relating my situation to other problems going on in the world. Second choice my eldest sister, I know she will understand. A year earlier she was out of a job for six months; however, I hesitate to tell her because she is a worrier. She has a habit of making everyone's problem her own, I didn't want to add anything to her plate because she always seems to have more going on than she can handle. As fate would have it, the decision was partially made for me. My mom called to see how my day was "I lost my job today" practically fell out of my mouth. Her response was comforting, "Son, God allows things to happen for a reason." It was also shocking because she didn't add her usual commentary of relating my situation to something that happened to someone else. She yells out to tell my dad and he grabs the phone and says, "It will be ok son." Before hanging up the phone my mother tells me, "Read the book of Job son, momma loves you. Good night."

It was around 9PM when I got off the phone. I realized I hadn't eaten since lunch, but I didn't have much of an appetite. I felt so empty on the inside, I had a major headache, and I felt alone. I went to my room to lie across the bed. Restless I got out of bed and decided to pick out something to wear for the next day, took a long shower hoping it would relax me. Of course, it doesn't work. Took an aspirin for my headache, prayed and got in the bed, tossed and turned all night; I slept very little. I kept trying to figure out what did I do wrong. "God, why did you allow this to happen to me?"

Day Two

I recall looking out the window before dawn, hoping the daylight wouldn't come because daylight was a reminder that another day had started and I didn't have a job to go to. I got out of the bed around eight and prepared to go meet Focused at the library. I found myself pacing around the room, decided to sit on the bed for about thirty minutes reflecting on my time at my old job. I blamed myself for my current situation, although I couldn't comprehend the reason why I was fired. I was reminded of the team I worked with and the great progress we made during my two years and nine months at Spirit Hospital. This stroll down memory lane was making me bitter and causing me to be depressed. Realizing this was an exercise in futility, I decided to move forward with my day. I couldn't keep up with time today. Before I knew it, it was 9 o'clock and I was not dressed. I texted Focused to let him know I was running an hour or more behind schedule. He replied "ok." Focused was very patient and understanding. I arrived at the library at 10:30. I forgot to bring my laptop and I didn't have a copy of my resume. I definitely was in a daze (fog). Focused brought some resume material for me to review and gave me a copy of his resume to use as a guide. We spent an hour on the library's computer looking for positions then we headed to lunch. It had been about 24 hours since I had eaten but I didn't have an appetite.

On the way home, I received a call from another friend, Reality Check. Reality Check called in response to a text I sent to him the day before. "Hey Evolving, this is Reality Check, man I know exactly what you going through. Man, it took me almost three years to find a full-time position. I want you to know man I am here if you need anything. I replied, "Thanks man." Reality Check added, "Dude you need to put your house on the market immediately, get rid of any unnecessary expenses. Man it is going to be a long winter, prepare for the worst. It will probably take you at least a year to find another job." I responded, "I am not ready to make all those decisions right now, I have some leads and I have faith I will have a job within three months. Reality Check responded, "Man don't be like them old folks and rely strictly on your faith. Put your house on the market by the end of the week, get a deferment on your student loan, convert some of your 401k into cash, spend your days and night applying for jobs online, and review the list of 300 jobs I forwarded you." I allowed my friend to finish his comments then I responded, "I appreciate your advice, but I think the worse thing I could do in this situation is to change to my daily life too quickly. I have made a number of the changes you recommended. I have endured a lot over the last two days and I need to maintain as much normalcy in my life as I can. Making all of the immediate changes you suggest at one time would set me back." Reality Check's response was: "Man you need to be realistic and put that house on the market, do what I say. I know what I am talking about." I replied, "Good night man." As I hung up the phone, I told myself I will only communicate with Reality Check by text until I get a job. I need to hear messages of hope right now, not fear and despair.

I hear a welcomed sound my stomach is growling, my appetite is back. I decided to prepare a quick meal and watch "Hangover" on cable. After the movie, I spent a couple of hours updating my resume. The time on my computer showed 11:30pm, it was a good time to shut down for the day. I turned off the computer, took a shower, read the 23rd Psalm. After reading the chapter, I slowly began to let go the feelings of shame, frustration, anger, defeat and fear and replaced them with thoughts of peace, victory, boldness and wholeness. I realized some things in life just happen, reliving the moments will not change a thing. I am thankful God gave spoke to my heart like he did David's in the 23rd Psalm. I said a prayer and fell asleep. "Who wouldn't serve a God like that?" Amen.

Day Three

I arose early Wednesday morning from a peaceful night rejuvenated and resolute, un-afraid of the daylight, ready to embrace the day. I thanked God for a new day and a new start. Throughout the night God spoke to my conscience, calmed my fears and allowed me to understand that he has allowed the enemy to test me but his blessings and mercy would cover me. My assurance was reinforced after I read the story of Job. I was also reminded that Jesus bore the cross but arose victorious from the grave with all power in his hands. I didn't awake with all power but I woke up with a reassurance that God was working for my good. I spent the day reaching out to contacts, had lunch with a friend, filled out applications online, meditated and prayed before heading to bed.

I realize the blessings I will gain and have gained from this experience are far greater than what the enemy thought he took. This moment signals for me a great change of direction in my life. In the past, God has elevated me to positions I didn't think I would have and my enemies didn't think I deserved. I sit in anticipation of what miraculous thing he is going to do next in my life. I am willing to do and go wherever he leads me without fear or reservation. To God be the glory.

Mom's Messages

1. Your fears can't be greater than your faith.
2. Don't focus on what you have lost focus on what you will gain.
3. Each Day is a gift full of promise and possibility.
4. When the enemy enters into your life, elevate your praise.
5. Recognize when your fence is being removed.
6. To move forward without bitterness, spend more time rejoicing over the rise and less time reliving the fall.

A prayer of confirmation

Thank you God for your comfort and your favor, continue to guide my steps so I won't stray. Let my reactions and actions toward my current situation serve as a visual testimony to those who need to see an example of your strength, courage, humility and faith. God grant me your peace that passes all understanding, let me receive the message this experience is to teach me. In your name I pray, Amen…

Recognition

"And we know that all this work together for good to them that love God, to them who are the called according to his purpose" (Romans8:28 KJV)

Growing up life wasn't always easy but God had a way of making our burdens light. Although there was seven of us (mom, dad, two brothers, two sisters and me) living in a three bedroom apartment in a public housing community, crime and drugs abound, a few trees, very little grass, no car, or health insurance, being described by society as underprivileged, one would think I didn't have a good childhood. Not so, I was very happy. My adult self would describe me as being blessed. I have two of the best parents in the world, we went to bed with a full belly every night, my mom sung gospel songs and read to us each night before bed, my dad kept a roof over our heads, and we were always clean. At the time I wasn't mature to understand the grace and mercy of God; He took the little we had and made much. There are countless times growing up I saw God show up and bless in a manner only he could; however, there is one period in my childhood that really stands out.

I was twelve years old my father lost his job approximately six months before this incident occurred. I recall this being a rough time for the family but it was also a time when God's provisions for us manifested through the acts of our relatives and friends. Our phone service was disconnected, but our neighbors were great they allowed us to use their phone whenever we needed to make a call. Often there would be a knock on the front door from neighbors informing us that either my cousins or aunt had a left message for us. While waiting for the government to process my parents' food stamp request, my cousin and my aunt brought us food from their cabinets, refrigerators and freezers. We never missed a meal.

Christmas that year was really different. A few weeks earlier, my parents told us they would not be able to buy us anything for Christmas. I was saddened by the news and wasn't looking forward to Christmas day. My mom refused to let our circumstance put a damper on what was always the family's favorite holiday. The day after my parents broke the news we put up the Christmas tree and decorated the house as we had done in years past. The only thing missing that year was presents, but my mom had an answer for that as well. We wrapped the gifts we received from the previous Christmas and placed them under the tree.

On Christmas Eve the house was full of activity, Christmas music was playing on the radio and the air was filled with wonderful aromas. My mom and aunt were in the kitchen putting the finishing touches on the Christmas feast. Actually my mom was preparing the Christmas feast, my aunt came over to keep her company and to ensure my mom cooked her three layer chocolate cake and a three layer apple jelly cake. Around 9pm, my mom told my brothers and me it was time to get ready for bed. An hour later I was lying in the bed looking at the ceiling, I couldn't fall asleep. In years past the anticipation of running downstairs finding boxes with my name on the tags and tearing them open to find out what I got was almost more than I could bear. I would lay there wishing the hours would pass.

It was our family's tradition to get up around four o'clock on Christmas morning to open gifts. My sisters would come wake my brothers and me. We would go over to my parent's room, knock on their door to wake them and then run downstairs to the living room to open gifts. This Christmas Eve I couldn't fall asleep because I had anxiety about how would I react when I got down stairs and there would be no new presents for me to open.

Apparently the rest of the family felt the same way, my sisters didn't come to our room until six o'clock and my parents were slow to rise that morning as well. Once everyone was gathered in the living room my mom said a prayer, she thanked God for all of us being together, safe and sound. She then led the family in singing happy birthday to Jesus. After singing, we opened the presents. All of the presents under the tree weren't from last Christmas. My sisters, brothers and I had saved money during the year; we were able to buy our parents and each other small gifts. After opening the presents, we put on clothes so we could go outside to play. Somehow my mom convinced the city to place barricades at both ends of our block for the day. All the kids in the neighborhood came to our street to skate and ride their bikes. My mom passed out fruit and cookies. My cousins and aunt came over that evening for dinner. I recall eating all day and I played until I was exhausted. This was a Christmas I will never forget.

Mom's Messages

1. **Acceptance of what is will give you peace in the valleys of life.**
2. **Find value in what you have and you will live a life of contentment.**
3. **Showing love for others without reservation.**

And The Blessings Keep Coming

Psalm 121:1-2King James Version (KJV)
121 I will lift up mine eyes unto the hills,
from whence cometh my help.
² My help cometh from the Lord, which made heaven and earth.

Prior to my dad finding a full-time job, he worked part-time as a waiter at several restaurants. My mom began selling homemade cookies and cakes to help keep the family a float.(My mother is a great cook, she is one of those individuals who can go in the kitchen with a bag of flour and a chicken and come out the kitchen an hour later with a gourmet meal. Her sweet potato pies and caramel cakes are second to none.) One day the neighbor from across the street came over to our house, she told my mom she was going to the dog track. She asked my mom did she want to place a bet on a race, my mom told the neighbor thanks but no thanks. "Are you sure girl, you don't have to send but a few dollars?" the neighbor replied. After a few moments of pondering her decision, my mom went to her room and brought back six dollars that she took from her cookie and cake sales and gave it to the neighbor. The neighbor asked "Girl, what race do you want to play and what numbers?" My mom looked at me and asked for a number. I told my mom three numbers and the race to play the numbers in; she wrote the information down and gave it to the neighbor. Later that night, someone knocked on the front door, my mom opened the door. It was our neighbor she came over to inform my mom that the numbers she sent to the dog track came in. Everyone was elated. My mom thanked the neighbor and gave her some of the winnings. It turns out the winnings were enough to take care of the past due bills.

While writing this chapter, I asked myself the question: why did I think winning money from a bet was a blessing from God? My answer is: In my thirteen year old mind, this was God's answer to my prayer and by my definition it was a blessing. Today, I know God as a provider and a sustainer and I know his promise is he will meet our every need. While I don't rely on him to sustain me through taking a risk on gambling, I know without a doubt he does and will work through unlikely sources to make sure needs are met. The word of God says he will give you the desires of your heart and he will. In this walk of faith I am journeying on I have come to understand if we focus on living our lives according to God's will, the desires of your heart and his will for us are one in the same.

Mom's Messages

1. **Favor is when God's will trumps human logic.**
2. **God is a way maker; he makes a way out of no way.**
3. **Before you give up, give hope another chance.**

God Is At Work!

1 Corinthians 2:9-11
New King James Version (NKJV)
⁹ But as it is written:
"Eye has not seen, nor ear heard,
Nor have entered into the heart of man
The things which God has prepared for those who love Him."[a]
¹⁰ But God has revealed *them* to us through His Spirit. For the Spirit searches all things, yes, the deep things of God. ¹¹ For what man knows the things of a man except the spirit of the man which is in him? Even so no one knows the things of God except the Spirit of God

Throughout my life I have heard the question: Where is God? To be honest, I have asked this question myself. As I have matured, and experienced the up and downs of life, I am convinced God is everywhere. Nothing in our lives, including work, is excluded from his purview. Scripture reminds us, God is at work in all things for our good. So that is my answer, God is **everywhere**.

I can recall vividly the first time I recognized God interceding in my work life, I had recently obtained a bachelor's degree in business and was working two jobs, by day I was a clerk at a local bank by night a customer-service clerk at a music store. The clerk position at the bank was really boring to say the least. My major job function was making copies and distributing the documents to the appropriate locations. I had very little interaction with the other employees and often found myself looking at my watch hoping the day would go by faster.

One day during my lunch break my mom called. She called to inform me about a dream she had. In her dream, I told her I had acquired a job at Major General Hospital. During our conversation I kept interjecting, telling her I didn't have much time. "Ok, I will make a long story short" she replied. After she finished recapping the "whole dream" she concluded with her interpretation of the dream. "Son, you should go to the Human Resources department at Major General Hospital and apply for a position." I told my mom I had applied for several positions with Major General Hospital in the past and never received a call back. My mom wasn't deterred by my weak attempt to get her off the phone. She talked right passed my response, as if I had never spoken. She quickly said again, "I dreamed you got a job at MAJOR GENERAL HOSPITAL, you should go fill out an application." I knew this was an argument I would not win, and considering I only had fifteen minutes remaining for my lunch break I conceded. "Mom, I will go to MGH to fill out an application. Talk to you later, love you." In hind sight, I am not really sure if I went to fill out the application because I believed my mom's dream or if I was simply being obedient. At any rate, I am forever grateful for

God speaking to my mother through a dream and for my mom having the wisdom to share God's message with me.

During lunch the next day, I went to the human resources department at MGH. I searched the job board seeking a position befitting my skills and education. After a few moments perusing the vacant jobs list I spotted the job for me: a junior accounting position. I completed the application, walked over to the reception area and gave the application to the lady behind the desk. I remember telling myself as I exited the building, "My chances of getting this job are slim to none at best."

It had been two weeks of cautious yet waning optimism before I received the call from MGH. "May I speak to Evolving?" It was the human resource representative, Memory Lane. I couldn't tell you the number of times I had mentally braced myself to read, *"Thank you for your interest in a career opportunity with MGH, but the position was offered to another candidate."* Nevertheless, here I was listening to Memory Lane inquire about the application I had submitted two weeks earlier. Before I could process what was happening, the phone call had ended. The only words I remember from the conversation was Memory Lane saying she was scheduling me for another interview in two weeks with the hiring manager. I spent the time leading up to the second interview doing mock interviews with some of my family members and scouring the internet for questions the interviewer may ask. I also did some research to find out if MGH was financially stable, the number of employees, annual income, annual patient visits. I knew this interview could be the break I needed and I was not going to leave anything to chance.

Finally the big day arrived. It was a pleasant autumn day the leaves had changed colors and had begun falling from the trees. It was sunny, no a cloud in sight, the temperature was around seventy degrees. I remember this day so vividly because I had the distinct feeling the leaves weren't the only thing changing. I was changing also, transitioning from a care free college student to a professional. I entered the building with a great degree of confidence. My shoes were shined. I chose to wear a dark blue suit and my new red and blue tie, a starched white shirt. You could say I had my swag on. After entering the lobby, I went to the receptionist desk. "Good morning, I have an appointment to see Ms. Lane." The receptionist replied, "What is your name?" "I am Evolving", I replied. "Thank you sir, I will tell Ms. Lane you are here." After a few minutes, a young lady entered the lobby. "Are you Mr. Evolving?" "Yes I am", I replied. I greeted her with a smile and a firm hand shake. During the interview Memory Lane asked me a series of questions. I made sure my replies were succinct and audible. I also made sure I made eye contact with her often.

Memory Lane asked "What career goals do you have for yourself?" I replied, "Are you referring to short-term or long-term goals?" "What's your five year plan?" "I see myself in a management role within the hospital." In some instances, I repeated Memory Lane's question as part of my response to make sure she knew I was listening. After a series of situational and career oriented questions, Memory Lane arose from her desk to thank me for coming. "Ms. Lane you look very familiar to me, I feel like we have met before." Looking surprised she replied, "Did you go to Next Level high school?" "No", I replied. Then it came to me, "Keep-Looking-Up Elementary school?" I asked. Memory Lane grinned and replied, "Fourth grade…Ms. Green's class." We began to talk about other classmates we've encountered through the years and recalled some of the fun times we had in Ms. Green's class. After completing our walk down memory lane, Ms. Lane told me she would follow up with me in a few weeks or so with details about my interview with the hiring manager in the finance department. As I got on the elevator, the conversation I had with my mother several weeks earlier came rushing back to me. My thoughts had changed entirely I just might get this job.

Immediately after work I prepared a thank you note for Memory Lane, I wanted her to know how grateful I was. As mama always says, "Tell people thank you when they do something for you because nobody owes you anything". In my life, I've learned that sometimes God uses other people to deliver messages to us because we may not be spiritually in tune to recognize his voice.

About two or three weeks passed and I hadn't heard anything from Memory Lane or the manager of the hiring department. After getting a little impatient, I called Memory Lane to ask her if I was still being considered for the job. She replied "yes." The process was taking a little longer than normal because the hiring manager was out on vacation for a week. She assured me she would give the manager a call that day and follow-up with me after she had spoken to him. As promised, the next day I received a call from Ms. Lane, telling me that she spoke with the manager of the department and he wanted to interview me for the Junior Accountant's position. I wrote down the date, time and location of my second interview and thanked Memory Lane again for all her help. My second interview proved to be just as memorable as my first. As I recall, my second interview took place the week before Thanksgiving. I arrived at the building where my interview would take place a few minutes early. As I opened the door to enter the office, I could see the reflection of a guy getting up from his desk. He was coming to see who was entering the office. Much to my surprise, it was one of my good friends, better than that I would eventually be the best man in his wedding. I knew Calm-n- Collected aka C&C worked for Major General Hospital, but I didn't know he worked in the Finance department. C&C greeted me, "Hey man, what are you doing here?"

I have an interview with Mr. Middle-of-the-Road, I replied. After we spent a few moments catching up with each other, my friend told me to have a seat and he would tell Mr. Middle-of-the-Road, the Reimbursement Manager I was there. The Reimbursement Manager came up to the reception area, my friend introduced him to me and me to him. "Mr. Middle-of-the-Road, this is Evolving, he and I went to The University together." The Reimbursement Manager, Mr. Middle-of-the-Road not being one for small talk politely ended the conversation quickly, escorted me to his office, asked me to have a seat and immediately started to ask questions. Mr. Middle-of-the-Road's questions were pretty standard. He asked: why did I apply for the position? What did I see myself doing in five years? He also asked me some situational questions. Mr. Middle-of-the-Road concluded with asking, "Evolving do you have any questions?" I replied "yes". "Sir, how long do you think it will be before you make a decision?" Mr. Middle-of-the-Road's replied, "You should hear something by next week".

After twenty minutes or so, I emerged from his office feeling confident I would get the job. My confidence was fueled by all of the evidence that God revealed to me. The first evidence was the dream, secondly there was only one Junior Accountant's position available, I was a childhood classmate of the HR representative and finally one of my best friends worked in the same department. I prepared a thank you letter that night for Mr. Middle-of-the-Road and mailed it to him the next day.

The next week I received a call from Memory Lane, the HR representative with Major General Hospital. Memory Lane called to offer me the Junior Accountant's position with Major General. Although the job was an entry level position and paying an entry level salary, I was overjoyed with the news. All I wanted was a chance to prove myself and God heard my prayer. I literally felt the pressure being lifted from me.

Mom's Messages

1. **God is speaking to you, slow down and listen.**
2. **Imagine what you desire with your dreams; have what you desire by working.**
3. **Put your shoes on God will direct your footsteps.**

Retrospection

Matthew 6:31-32 New International Version (NIV)
³¹ So do not worry, saying, 'What shall we eat?' or 'What shall we drink?' or 'What shall we wear?' ³² For the pagans run after all these things, and your heavenly Father knows that you need them.

Prior to the file clerk position at the local bank, I worked as a bookkeeper for a small medical tubing manufacturing company. The company employed about 15 workers. My office was a small windowless box located in the front of the building. The office reeked of cigarette smoke; employees were allowed to smoke in the break-room. I worked under the ever watchful eye of my boss' wife. In her eyes, I could never do enough to satisfy her. I worked sixty hours a week, the more tasks I completed the more tasks I was expected to complete. The job responsibilities read like a grocery list, process bi-weekly payroll checks, pay local, county and state payroll tax, prepare the monthly bank reconciliation, order supplies, pay the bills, conduct weekly inventory in the warehouse, run errands for the boss and his wife, meet with vendors. It didn't take me long to figure out that this was a job I wouldn't want to do my whole career. What I didn't know was my boss' wife was working behind the scenes to free up my future so I can find that perfect job. In other words, I got terminated.

The day prior to me being relieved of my duties, my boss' wife entered my office as I was preparing to leave after another very long and trying day. Just like the days before, my boss' wife came in to scrutinize my work and tell me what else needed to be done before I departed for the day. This was normal behavior for her and on previous occasions I would listen to her and respond to her demands by either staying late or adding the tasks to the next day's responsibilities. This day was different. "Where do you think you are going?" she asked. I replied, "If my car cranks, I am going home." I think on this day I had reached my limit. She was visibly bothered by my response. I can't recall all the choice words that flowed like water from her mouth, but after five minutes or so of letting me have it, she exited the room. I finished gathering my belongings and left for the day. The next day my boss called me to his office around mid-morning and you can guess what happened.

After six months on this roller coaster, the ride came to an abrupt but welcomed end. Can we say emancipation? I am not boasting about being fired, but I would be lying if I say I wasn't relieved. All my life I was taught never to quit, but my philosophy today is "it is ok to leave a bad play before the curtain closes". In other words, if I ever find myself in a similar situation I would not hesitate leaving because no job or task is worth sacrificing your peace of mind or health for.

After thanking my boss for the opportunity, I went to my car. I sat there for a moment trying to figure out my next move. I decided to go to the mall to buy a tie for my next job and then I got lunch. While eating a chicken sandwich, fries and lemonade for lunch, the reality of me be unemployed took center stage in my mind. How would I pay my car note, student loans and other expenses? Immediately I was overwhelmed. I quickly gathered myself, focused on securing employment and the next day I went to a temporary agency where I was assigned a position with Moon Bank.

Mom's Messages

1. **Dust your shoes off so you don't dirty up the floor.**
2. **Be thankful God knows best.**
3. **Sometimes you have to close the window to keep the flies out.**

Stretching Out On Faith (A Yearning On The Inside)

2 Corinthians 9:8 New International Version (NIV)
⁸ And God is able to bless you abundantly, so that in all things at all times, having all that you need, you will abound in every good work.

I worked for MGH for six years, while there I was received one promotion, learned a lot, endured a lot and prayed a lot. Approximately two months before leaving MGH, I received a call from a business associate, A-matter-of-Fact. "Hello Evolving this is A-matter-of-Fact, how are you?"

"I am good, how are you A-matter-of-Fact?"

"I am good as well. I am not going to hold you long. I was calling to see if you would be interested in working for me as an A/R supervisor at The Hospital."

"Thanks for thinking of me A-matter-of-Fact but I have never supervised anyone before. Will you give me some time to think about the offer?"

"I will give you some time, but I wouldn't have called you if I didn't think you couldn't do the job Evolving. Let me know soon because I need to fill this position as soon as possible."

"Thanks A-matter-of-Fact, talk to you soon."

What was wrong with me? The way things were going at work I should have accepted her offer at that very moment. I actually spent a week or two contemplating the idea of leaving MGH and going to work as a supervisor at The Hospital. The day I made my decision to call A-matter-of-Fact back to inquire about the position is still a vivid memory in my mind. It was a Monday, late Autumn; I woke up that morning with an empty feeling in my belly. The emptiness was not because I hadn't eaten. I think it was my spirit telling me I needed to change directions. In addition to the emptiness, I also felt dread. I didn't want to work for MGH anymore. I called the office to speak to my boss, Mr. Middle-of-the-Road. He didn't pick up the phone so I left him a message telling him I wasn't feeling well and wouldn't be in the office today, I picked up the phone to call A-matter-of-Fact. She answered. "Hi A-matter-of-Fact, this Evolving, how are you?" "I am good" she replied. "A-matter-of-Fact, I thought about the supervisor position you told me about some weeks ago, I am interested in the position." "Evolving, I offered the job to someone else." After hearing her response, I felt a big knot in my throat. "Excuse me, you ah offered the position to someone else??" I replied.

"Evolving, I told you I had to fill the position, I just made the offer this morning but the candidate told me he would have to think about the salary. I will call back to see if he has made up his mind."

"I hope this guy doesn't want the position because I am ready to leave this place." I replied. A-matter-of-Fact replied "I will call you back after I get his reply."

"Thanks A-matter-of-Fact, talk to you later."

A couple days passed (it seemed like weeks). Finally, I received a call from A-matter-of-Fact.

"Evolving, this is A-matter-of-Fact the other candidate turned the position down. If you are serious about this opportunity come by the HR department to fill out an application today. After you complete the application, come by my office and I will formally interview you."

"I am definitely interested in the position, A-matter-of-Fact. I am on the way over to the HR department now and will stop by your office afterwards. Thanks again for the opportunity, I will not disappoint you." A-matter-of-Fact replied "I know you won't Evolving, see you soon."

I arrived at A-matter-of-Fact's office around 11:00AM. She was at her desk reading something on her computer. The door was opened, but I knocked. A-matter-of-Fact looked up from her computer and invited me in. She got straight down to business. A-matter-of-Fact explained the responsibilities of the job to me as well as her expectations. Because A-matter-of-Fact was aware of my hesitancy about supervising most of her questions were scenarios concerning employee performance and behavior. A-matter-of-Fact asked "What would you do if you had an employee who was not productive and a nuisance to the department?"

My response was "I would initially counsel the employee about the inappropriate behavior. If the problems continued, I would write the employee up for the offense. The employee would be put on an action plan if little or no improvement was made." A-matter-of-Fact nodded her head and continued her What-ifs. After another fifteen minutes of questions, A-matter-of-Fact stated she would contact HR and they would follow up with me regarding next steps. The next day I received a call from the HR manager offering me the AR supervisor position with The Hospital. I graciously accepted the offer. The HR manager quoted the salary, orientation dates and times and informed me that letter in the mail confirming what she said in our meeting.

Mom's Messages

1. **Listen to your inner voice.**
2. **You never know who will offer you assistance, be kind to everyone.**
3. **The world is small; establish a good working relationship with fellow employees. A co-worker today may be your boss tomorrow.**
4. **If you have thirst, it is good to drink from a familiar stream.**

Change Is Inevitable

(Ecclesiastes 3: 1-8)There is a time for everything, and a season for every activity under the heavens:[2] a time to be born and a time to die, a time to plant and a time to uproot,[3] a time to kill and a time to heal, a time to tear down and a time to build,[4] a time to weep and a time to laugh, a time to mourn and a time to dance,[5] a time to scatter stones and a time to gather them, a time to embrace and a time to refrain from embracing,[6] a time to search and a time to give up, a time to keep and a time to throw away,[7] a time to tear and a time to mend, a time to be silent and a time to speak,[8] a time to love and a time to hate, a time for war and a time for peace. (Holy Bible, New International Version®, NIV® Copyright © 1973, 1978, 1984, 2011 by Biblica, Inc.®)

The first year on my new job with "The Hospital" was filled with ups and down but I am glad to say there were more ups than downs. This was a very joyous time, personally and professionally. In June of my second year on the job, I bought my first house. All of my siblings were doing well and my parents bought their first home as well. I felt like things were clicking for me. The staff at work was working together as a team, we were meeting or exceeding department goals, my boss was tough but fair, I got off work every evening at a decent hour and for the most part life in general was pretty drama-free. This was the first time in my career I felt as though my contributions were impacting the organization in a visible and distinct way:

employee morale was up, turnover was down, processes were streamlined, and cash collections were up. The many hours of mentoring I received from A-matter-of-Fact, the eight week management classes I took, system training and excel training courses, one on one time with staff, and last but not least the four years of mistreatment I endured at MGH all contributed to the moment.

Fast forward one year, and my manager walked into my office with a concerned look on her face. I asked her if there was anything I could do for her. She responded by saying she was there to inform me of a decision the corporate office had made in regards to our day to day operations. In an effort to streamline operations and reduce redundancy in the system, the company felt it would be in its best interest to create regional centralized business offices throughout the country. The regional business offices would be responsible for providing the services currently being performed at each of the company's 30 or more hospitals in thirteen states. "A-matter-of-Fact, what does this mean for me and my department?" A-matter-of-Fact replied, "Evolving your department as well as some other areas within my division will be eliminated." Initially, I had no response at all. It took me a few moments to gather my thoughts then I asked "A-matter-of-Fact, what is the timeline for the transition?" A-matter-of-Fact responded, "The areas are scheduled to close in December and the regional office would take over operations the first of the year."

She was going make the announcement to the entire staff at the next departmental meeting.

During the meeting as you can imagine, emotions were running high and questions were being thrown around like grenades. A-matter-of-Fact called for calm in the room and explained what would happen in the days to come. I must commend A-matter-of-Fact for remaining calm and in control. I believe if she had panicked or shown any fear, the staff would have fed off of her energy and the next six months would have been really difficult for everyone affected. I learned a great lesson about leadership that day. A good leader is one that maintains their composure and resolve during difficult situations. They have an amazing ability to make one feel everything will work out. During the departmental meeting, affected employees were told they would receive incentive pay if they continued their employment with "The Hospital" until the end of the year. In addition, corporate brought in career consultants to discuss everything from interviewing to resume writing. The corporate office also held interviews at the facility. They scheduled time for the Atlanta regional director and the New Orleans regional director to come to "The Hospital" and interview the staff affected by the transition for positions within their respective offices. I walked around day after day with a laser like focus trying not to focus on the transition. For some reason, I thought if the staff performed at a higher level over the next five months corporate would change its mind and let things stay as they were. I was definitely in a state of denial. In fact, my thoughts were so far removed from the reality of the situation that I had to be reminded by a friend of my impending joblessness. After being confronted with reality of the inevitable, I submitted an application to the Atlanta and New Orleans offices for a reimbursement management position. It never really dawned on me that I would have to move to another state and may have to sell my house. I began to experience feelings of anxiety. What would happen to me financially if I didn't find work soon? If I found a job in another city, how could I afford to rent an apartment and pay my mortgage?

First thing first, I concentrated on securing one of the management positions I applied for. After a month or so of researching the position and doing mock interviews with family and friends, I was told I would be granted interviews with the director of the Atlanta and New Orleans business office. Hearing this news turned on a light inside of me; my thoughts turned from pity and despair to anticipation and hope. My outlook on the whole situation immediately changed. My confidence level rose exponentially, doubt was replaced with assuredness. I knew I would land one of the management positions. It is so amazing how something so small as the invitation to interview changed my whole perspective. I was reminded of the scripture: **He said to them, "Because of your little faith. For truly, I say to you, if you have faith like a**

grain of mustard seed, you will say to this mountain, 'Move from here to there,' and it will move, and nothing will be impossible for you." Matthew 17:20 ESV I knew God was up to something and this was going to be another mountain moving experience in my life. God was going to move as he had done in the past.

While I was preparing myself to move forward, I realized as a leader within the organization I needed to focus a great deal of attention on keeping the staff's spirits lifted. Instead of having staff meetings bi-weekly, I began having less formal staff meetings on a weekly basis. The meetings were less structured than normal, no agenda. Most of what was discussed was initiated by the employees. Allowing them a controlled forum to express their feelings, would reduce or eliminate the need to have numerous informal conversations throughout the day which could affect morale and productivity. Being present, I was able to subtly influence the direction of the conversation. When an employee would speak negatively about the organization or the dismantling of the department I would offer a comment about what we had accomplished together and how each person would go on to accomplish great things in the future.

Finally the day of reckoning was near, I received an e-mail regarding the dates and times I would be interviewed. The interviews were scheduled two days a part. My first interview was scheduled with the director of the New Orleans office. I was prepared and I was eager to share my thoughts with the interviewer.

I must say after the introductions were completed and the first few questions were asked I knew I wouldn't get the job. Surprisingly I was totally ok with that. There was no chemistry between the interviewer and me. I felt awkward. In the back of my mind I thought to myself, the second interview has to go better than this one. As fate would have it, my interview with the director of the Atlanta office went much smoother. As I entered the room, the interviewer stood up from her seat. "Good morning you are Evolving, correct?" Yes, I replied. "Nice to meet you, I am Happy-to-be-here, please have a seat." Ms. Happy-to-be-here smiled during the interview. She described the job to me, thanked me for applying, and began asking me questions. Although I knew I had to land this job, I didn't feel pressured. The interviewer and I clicked immediately, I thought during the interview I would like to work for this person. As I do after any interview, I sent thank you letters to both ladies thanking them for taking time out to speak with me regarding an opportunity within their departments.

I can't recall exactly how much time passed, but I am sure it wasn't more than a few weeks before I received a letter in the mail from the New Orleans office. Normally I am nervous at moments like this, but for some reason, I opened the envelope right away. The letter read, "Another candidate was chosen for the position you applied for, we thank you for your interest in seeking a career opportunity with this organization."

Not a big surprise to me, actually I think I was a little relieved. A week later, I received a phone call from the HR representative for the Atlanta regional office. She was calling to offer me the reimbursement manager position. I asked a few questions, but ultimately accepted the position. The representative said I would receive an official offer letter in the mail detailing the offer. "Thank God." For the first time in a while, I reflected on all that had happened. Moments before the call, my reality was "a soon-to-be-out-of-work supervisor but God had other plans. God again had shown me favor. He had provided me with a new job which was a promotion including a nice salary increase, a signing bonus and a relocation allowance. "Who wouldn't serve a GOD like that?" I smiled, took a deep breath and began to cast my thoughts on what life would be like living in another city. The next day, I went to my boss' office to tell her about the position. She congratulated me and told me she knew I would do well. The month leading up to my departure was full of mixed emotions. I was sad to be leaving the people I had developed a bond with, uncertain about my ability to create a stronger or similar bond with my new employees and mainly I was terrified of what life would be like in a different city; however, the thought of me going somewhere new, meeting new people, having new experiences, overcoming new challenges I was hopeful, joyous and grateful.

Mom's Messages

1. If you gain weight, buy larger pants.
2. Whatever the season, God will be with you.
3. Take a chance there are many roads that will get you home.

A Prayer for Work

Oh Lord, bless my efforts so they may be
adequate to meet the needs of the day.
Guide my feet and hands in thy service.
Continue to let your favor fall
fresh on me each day.
Keep my eyes ever on the cross to remind
me of your ultimate sacrifice.
Thank you for what you have done
and what you will do today.
Bless my efforts as a leader and use
me in your service so your will may be
done on earth as it is in Heaven…
AMEN

Things Change. Deal With It

> Jeremiah 29:11 New International Version (NIV)
> 11 For I know the plans I have for you," declares
> the Lord, "plans to prosper you and not to harm
> you, plans to give you hope and a future.

The transition from Birmingham to Atlanta wasn't as difficult as I thought it would be (I owe my family and friends for that). A few weeks before the move, my friends gave me a grand going away party. I danced all night. The next weekend, my parents invited the family over to their house for a feast in my honor. Like every special occasion, my mom cooked enough food for an army. The menu consisted of my favorites: green beans, chicken and dressing, ribs, grilled chicken, macaroni and cheese, corn on the cob, collard greens, cranberry sauce, and caramel cake and sweet potato pies for desert.

On moving day, ten people showed up to help. We cleaned the old house, loaded the moving truck, two cars and headed to Atlanta. The drive to the new place took approximately three hours. Once there, we immediately got to work unloading. After a couple hours of focused effort, the place was beginning to look like home. While my mom and cousins were washing dishes and putting up pictures, I went out to get lunch for everyone. We fellowshipped over fried chicken, rolls, coleslaw, and fries. After eating the crew was ready to hit the road but not before we played cards. An hour later my dad announced, "It is getting late, we should be getting on the road." My older brother responded, "Yeah it's about that time, I have to go to work in the morning." Shortly after the announcement, everyone gave me a hug, said so long, and headed back home. The days following the move, phone calls from family and friends made me feel home was always near. In addition, my older sister lived about twenty-five minutes from me, she appointed herself as my guide, protector. For real she was definite clutch in helping me stay focused; she takes her role as big sister very serious.

The first day on the new job I was anxious and my head was full of thoughts: Would I be liked by the staff? Could I do the job? I was a nervous wreck. On top of that, my boss informed me I would be responsible for providing support services for up to seven hospitals, not three as I was initially told. One major thing I learned about working in corporate America is things change quickly and you have to be ready to change also.

My first day was jammed packed with activity. I started the day off with a meeting in my boss' office, from there she escorted me to my office. I was then taken to the HR department to complete my benefit and payroll documents. The HR representative gave me a tour of the building. I was introduced to my staff and other people in the building. I sat in on a few meetings, had lunch, taken back to my office around three o'clock where I would spent the remainder of the day setting up my voicemail, answering questions from the staff while also trying to track down the Information systems' guy to set up my computer. The chaos didn't end with my first day, the days to follow proved to be even more chaotic.

Tuesday morning I was greeted by numerous e-mails and voicemails from CFOs requesting a status on their daily cash reports. I reached out to each CFO and explained we were having system issues and I was working to get the issue resolved as soon as possible. I assured them the problem would be fixed by mid-week. Fortunate for me, each CFO stated the Wednesday would be ok. After putting out this fire, my manager came over to inform me that I would only have one supervisor and not three as we had previously discussed. (Two other lessons corporate America has taught me: believe what is done and not what is said, the second is things change, deal with it.) I must say these were stressful times; I got into work at 7am and left work around 7pm. I had very little time to explore the city. The only landmarks I was intimately familiar with were the gas station, the grocery store and the Wal-Mart which was about six blocks from my apartment. I was exhausted and disconnected from everyone. Did I make the right decision?

Mom's Messages

1. To find out where your journey will lead, you may have to travel on unpaved roads.
2. Family and friends are like good soul food. They provide comfort.
3. Life ain't easy son; you just have to deal with it.

A Place For Me

> 11For I know the plans I have for you," declares the Lord, "plans to prosper you and not to harm you, plans to give you hope and a future. 12Then you will call on me and come and pray to me, and I will listen to you. 13You will seek me and find me when you seek me with all your heart. 14I will be found by you," declares the Lord, "and will bring you back from captivity. I will gather you from all the nations and places where I have banished you," declares the Lord, "and will bring you back to the place from which I carried you into exile."(Jeremiah 29: 11-14, NIV)

After a month on the job, I received a call from a familiar person. It was A-matter-of-Fact, my boss from "The Hospital", she called to check on me. After we exchanged pleasantries, I told her I was extremely busy and a felt bit overwhelmed. "That's normal you will be fine once you get familiar with you daily responsibilities." She replied. Before we ended the call, A-matter-of-Fact wanted to know if I would be interested in working with her again. I emphatically replied "yes". "I may have a Reimbursement manager position available soon; I don't have many details to share at the moment. I will call you back when I know more." "THANKS A-matter-of-Fact, I look forward to your call."

A couple of weeks passed and I received a follow-up call from A-matter-of-Fact. "Hello, may I speak with Evolving?" "This is Evolving." "Hi, this is A-matter-of-Fact. I won't keep you long, I am calling to offer you the reimbursement manager position I spoke to you about during our last conversation. Because you were displaced during the transition, I am offering you the first right to refuse." "Thanks for the call A-matter-of-Fact, I gladly accept the offer and look forward to working with you again." After the call, I walked over to my manager's office to inform her of the offer and my acceptance of the offer. She stated she was disappointed with my decision because things were just starting to go smoothly in my area and my leaving would stall progress. "I understand and I appreciate you for giving me this awesome opportunity; however, due to personal reasons also I am going leave." My manager responded, "I guess, I understand." As I worked out a thirty day notice my focus and my thoughts slowly turned towards returning home.

As I drove out of the apartment complex gates for the last time, I thought to myself "Who wouldn't serve a God like that?" God in his usual way had done the impossible for me again. Within a three month period of time not only did he provide me with a job when I needed one, the job was a promotion accompanied by a signing bonus and a relocation package. As favor would have it, I was allowed to keep the signing bonus, and relocation money, promotion. Return back to work in a familiar place, I was able to break my lease in Atlanta with no penalty and able to move back in my house... This experience along with the others before it helped strengthen my faith and understanding of God being my heavenly father. I knew without a shadow of doubt what my mom told me all of my life was true. God knows me by name, he even knows the number of hairs on my head and he will take care of his children. After this experience I vowed to be more faithful and avail myself to be of service to God wherever he would have me to go and do whatever he would have me to do. ("No eye has seen, no ear heard, and no mind has imagined what God has prepared for those who love Him." 1 Corinthians 2:9 (NLT)

Sunnyside-Up

After my return to "The Hospital", things went along with no major hiccups for about two years; however, the winds of change began to blow. One announcement would cause a chain reaction that would forever change my relationship with a co-worker and take my career to the next level. My director, A-matter-of-Fact called a meeting with all of her direct reports. During the meeting she told us she accepted a position as a regional director with corporate. A-matter-of-Fact also told us she was going to appoint Sunnyside-Up, one of the managers as the Interim Director. I was excited for A-matter-of-Fact and Sunnyside-Up. After the meeting, I congratulated both of them. A-matter-of-Fact stated she would be around for the next thirty days and beyond that she would visit our facility often because "The Hospital" was one of the hospitals in her region. In other words, we would still have to work with her, but not on a daily basis. Over the next thirty days A-matter-of-Fact worked very closely with Sunnyside-Up to insure a smooth transition. Of all the managers on staff, it was no surprise Sunnyside-Up was chosen. Sunnyside-Up was very bright and A-matter-of-Fact had been grooming her for this moment. Sunnyside-Up had an impeccable work ethic; she would arrive at work early and work late into the evening. She would be the first person to volunteer for assignments and would often accompany A-matter-of-Fact to meetings. Sunnyside-Up worked her way up through the ranks. She began her career in healthcare as a secretary. Sunnyside began working for "The Hospital" approximately two months before I did. Initially, Sunnyside and I met years earlier while she was working as A-Matter-of-Fact's secretary, but she and I had never had a real conversation.

On my first day Sunnyside was the first person to come by my office. "Good morning Evolving. Welcome aboard, let me know if you need anything." "Hi Sunnyside, thank you. I will definitely reach out to you if I need your help. What is your extension?" She replied, "9311. I am going to let you get settled, just stopped by to say hi. Have a good day!" I wished her a good day as well. Sunnyside spoke to each of my employees as she left my section. As time passed, she and I developed a great working relationship. We also became lunch buddies. We both enjoyed good food. I am sure the lunch hour staff of most restaurants within a five mile radius of the hospital knew us by name. One of the local bakeries in the area offered us discounts on pastries and food because we stopped by at least once a week. During my six year tenure with "The Hospital" I would call on Sunnyside many times for help with training my staff or assistance with developing a new process or creating a spreadsheet.

Weeks after Sunnyside was announced as the interim director she came by my office to chat about the transition. "Hi Evolving, you got a minute?" "Sure Sunnyside, come in and have a seat. What's going on?" Sunnyside replied, "Nothing much I just wanted to talk about the transition." "Sunnyside I think you will get the position on a permanent basis. I am very excited for you." "Thanks Evolving but there is no guarantee I will get the job. If I don't get it I would be happy if you got it. I could work for you. So Evolving are you going to apply for the director's role?" "I am not sure", I replied.

Some time later I spoke with A-Matter-of-Fact and she informed me the CFO converted the department from one department to two. Under the current structure, A-Matter-of-Fact was responsible for the registration and business office staff. The new structure would have a director for the registration staff and a director for the business office staff. "Evolving, have you applied for the director of registration position?" I replied, "No, I haven't made up mind." "If you don't apply Evolving, you definitely won't get the position. Don't count yourself out before you count yourself in." "Thanks A-Matter-of-Fact. I will complete and submit the application online tonight."

Shortly after I submitted my application, the vice president of human resources' secretary called me to set up an interview. I spent the night before the interview reading articles about patient registration and reviewing industry reports. I also memorized the department's organization chart as well as learned the primary functions of each area. This time my confidence level was high because I didn't have the pressure of feeling like I had to land a job because I already had one. In addition, the vice president and I knew each other so I didn't feel the added pressure of speaking to a stranger. The interview was more like a conversation between a mentor and mentee than an interview. The interviewer asked questions regarding my career goals. She also encouraged me to continue developing my skills by obtaining certifications and pursuing a master's degree. At the conclusion of the interview, the vice president told me the next step would be to interview with a panel of directors who would have an indirect or direct relationship with the director of registration, she wished me well and I went back to work.

Immediately after arriving back to the department, I went to Sunnyside's office to share my thoughts regarding the interview. I peeped in Sunnyside's door. "Hey, do you have a minute? I wanted to tell you about my interview." "C'mon in", Sunnyside replied. "I feel like it went really well, I was told the next step is to be interviewed by a panel. I am excited but also a little nervous." Sunnyside smiled "I think you will get the position because it isn't a difficult job to learn and you are good communicator." This certainly didn't sound like a comment I would expect to hear from my lunch buddy. In hind sight I really shouldn't have been surprised. Sunnyside had become distant and we had begun to communicate less since I told her I was going to apply for director of registration position. I thought

Sunnyside's attitude towards me changed because she wanted me to get use to things being different between us if she got the director's position. I was totally alright with that mind-set; I knew our work relationship would have to change if she became my boss. Honestly I think Sunnyside was a little resentful of the fact I was being giving an opportunity she thought I didn't deserve. This was her moment to shine and she was not up for sharing the lime-light. She was the one who had been groomed to be the director not me.

Moments before the panel interview began, my palms were sweaty, my heart beat increased and my mouth was dry. The interview was held in the executive boardroom which was located in hospital administration's suite. I entered the door of the administrative suite and greeted the receptionist there. I told her I was there for an interview in the boardroom. She stated they were expecting me and escorted me to the room where some of the members of the panel were already gathered. As my eyes scanned the room, I felt myself getting a little nervous because I didn't recognize any of the panel members. The facilitator greeted me and told me they were waiting on a few more people to arrive. It seemed like an hour but it was only ten minutes or so before the final members arrived. Introductions ensued. The panel consisted of department heads from various departments. During the introductions I made sure I made eye contact with each person as they spoke. Introductions were completed; the questioning began. Either I passed out during the interview or my body was on cruise control because the last thing I recall hearing was the facilitator saying: "that concludes our questions. Do you have any questions for us?" "Not at the moment, I like to thank each of you for taking the time to speak with me. If I have additional questions, may I reach out to each of you by e-mail?" Some members nodded their heads in the affirmative, the remaining members said, "yes".

Days after the interview I received a call from the CFO's assistant, she stated she was calling to set up a lunch meeting with me to discuss the director's position. I responded right away to avoid sounding like I was shocked, quite the contrary was true. I accepted the date and time the assistant gave me. I thanked her and ended the call. I met with Mr. Nobleman, the CFO for lunch as scheduled.

This was my first time having a one on one meeting with Mr. Nobleman so I didn't know what to expect. We both got our lunch and found a place to sit. "Evolving I asked you here because you are one of the finalist for the director of registration role. Why should you be offered the position? Several thoughts entered my head; I am so thankful God took those thoughts and translated them to the right words for Mr. Nobleman's ears. I responded, "Well Mr. Nobleman, I am glad you ask that question. Although, I have not worked in registration, my experience as an accountant, an A/R supervisor and Reimbursement manager would serve the department well. I will use my analytical skills to look at things from a different perspective, a perspective that a person with only patient registration experience will not be able to provide. I will offer new solutions to old problems." Mr. Nobleman asked a few more questions and the interview was over.

The next day I received a call from the Vice President of Human Resources. She offered me the position and I graciously accepted. Immediately after hanging up the phone, I went to A-Matter-of-Fact's office to tell her my exciting news. A-Matter-of-Fact celebrated with me and expressed how proud she was of me and she knew I would do a great job. I thanked her once again for all she had done for me through the years. I also told her she would be missed. I then guided my feet towards Sunnyside's office, where to my surprise the announcement of me getting the promotion garnered a less than jubilant reaction. I thought of all the people in the office who be excited for me Sunnyside certainly would be, especially when you consider the fact she was offered and accepted the business office director's role a couple of days earlier. At the time, I was a little caught up in the moment. I didn't really pay attention to her response to my news. During this particular conversation with Sunnyside, I shared my thoughts on the salary I was offered. I told her I was thrilled to be offered the position but I thought the compensation would be more. Sunnyside didn't offer a rebuttal to my statement.

Sometime after my conversation with Sunnyside, I spoke to one of my mentors about my new role. During that conversation, the mentor stated she overheard Sunnyside telling an individual in the office details of a conversation Sunnyside and I had about salary. My mentor also told me Sunnyside stated my attitude about my new role was negative. I told my mentor that was not the case. I went on to say how grateful I was for the opportunity. My mentor stated she felt that was not my intent; she said she only shared this information with me to caution me. After my conversation with my mentor, I reflected on what she told me. I was so disappointed in Sunnyside. For one, I didn't think she would repeat our conversation to someone else and secondly why would she tell someone details of our private conversation.

A couple of days after this incident, Sunnyside and I were invited by the administration team to dinner after work. The CEO wanted to celebrate the successful completion of another Joint Commission Survey. During the celebration, Sunnyside and I were introduced as the new directors of the business office and the director of patient registration. There was no honeymoon period for us. In a twinkling of an eye Sunnyside and I went from being buddies to being something far opposite of that. Sunnyside began to challenge me on everything. Every conversation turned into a debate. In Sunnyside's opinion, my department and I couldn't do anything right.

I was at my wits end trying to figure out how to restore my relationship with Sunnyside. I decided I would talk to Sunnyside about our relationship and discuss how we could work together as a team. I scheduled some time on her calendar. She agreed to the meeting. Sunnyside's office was located off campus. It was raining the day of our meeting so I parked in the parking deck because I didn't have an umbrella. Either Sunnyside had someone spying on me or she saw me drive up to the building. When I reached Sunnyside's office, I knocked on the door. "Hi Evolving." "Hello Sunnyside, how are you?" Instead of responding with how she was doing she said, "You can't park under the deck that is reserved for employees only." "Are you serious?" I replied. Sunnyside replied, "Yes I am serious." "Please accept my apology; I didn't have an umbrella so I parked under the deck. I didn't know it would pose a problem. At any rate, I wanted to meet to talk about our relationship. You have changed. You snap at me all the time, you constantly complain about my department, you never want to compromise. It's either your way or no way." Sunnyside responded, "I have not changed, I am the same way I have always been." At that moment, I felt like blinders were removed from my eyes. Sunnyside was right. I accepted her comments as a revelation. Eventually we learned to co-exist in our new roles but we never restored the relationship I thought we had.

Mom's Messages

1. When folks reveal who they really are, believe them and accept your new reality.
2. God's blessings for you are sufficient to meet your needs. Rejoice when you witness him bless someone else.
3. If God chooses to bless your neighbor, it does not diminish the blessings he has bestowed on you.
4. An old car or a new car can get you to your destination. Realize some people have no transportation at all. A blessing is a blessing, period.

Purpose And Provision

Psalm 37:25 New International Version (NIV)
²⁵ I was young and now I am old,
yet I have never seen the righteous forsaken
or their children begging bread.

After receiving my bachelor's degree in business, I worked as a clerk at a local bank. Although I was grateful to have a job, I knew I had to do more. It wasn't just about me; it was also about honoring my parents. They made tremendous sacrifices so my siblings and I could have a better life. My dad worked as a waiter for over thirty years, he was subjected to mistreatment and often looked at as less than because of the job he performed. Despite the conditions he worked in and the treatment he endured, he placed his family's needs above his pride. My dad taught me the value of hard work and the principles of being on time and being a man of your word. My dad was a good waiter, he did his job with dignity and respect.

As an adult, I've had the pleasure of working side by side with him when the catering service he worked for needed an extra person to work special events. In working with him, I got an up close and personal view of some of the treatment he had to endure all those years. People talked down to me or wouldn't talk to me or even look me directly in the eye. I felt like I was looked at as a machine and not as a person. As a child, I never heard my dad talk about the trials and tribulations he had on his job. I do recall overhearing my mom telling a family member how my dad was underpaid, talked down to and eventually terminated from a position because he was going to sign up to be a member of the union.

My mom made many sacrifices in her own right. My mom made the ultimate sacrifice for my siblings and I before we were born. She risked her freedom in hopes that my siblings and I could grow up in a world where our work performance and character would matter more than the color of our skin. My mom was a "foot soldier" during the Civil Rights movement. She was placed in jail with Dr. Martin Luther King Jr. during the sixties. In addition, my mom taught me how to love God, (share my time, talents and resources.) She also taught me to speak up for what is right and just. I recall one time she organized a boycott against the neighborhood grocery store owners because they had wrongly detained and accused several children of stealing from the store. The boycott was successful. After three weeks of picketing the store, the owners eventually met with my mom and other neighborhood leaders. The store owners agreed to change their policy and became more involved in the community. My mom taught me how to love my neighbor as I love myself. She also taught me the value of saving a part of what you earn. When I was eight years old my mom started a savings club for my brothers, four neighborhood boys and me. We raised money by washing cars, and selling hot dogs and sodas during the summer. The money we earned was put in a savings account and distributed to us in December.

MOM'S MESSAGES

1. **Money earned is more valuable than money given.**
2. **Faith strengthens your desire to persevere, perseverance strengthens character.**
3. **There is honor in doing a task well.**

In Transition

**Matthew 6:33 New International Version (NIV)
33 But seek first his kingdom and his righteousness, and all these things will be given to you as well.**

An e-mail sent from Hospital Administration read: Mr. Nobleman, CFO will be leaving the organization. We would like to thank him for his service and wish him well in his new role. Later that day Mr. Nobleman stopped by my office to tell me he accepted a position with a large healthcare system in another city. A month or so after his leaving, I learned the system director of registration position at Mr. Nobleman's new place of employment was vacant. The system director would be responsible for managing the registration staff at the system's three facilities. I called Mr. Nobleman to see how things were going and inquire about the position. During the conversation, Mr. Nobleman asked if I was interested in pursuing the opportunity. I asked him if I could give him a response in a day or so. He stated that would be fine, I thanked him for his time and told him I would be in contact soon. After I hung up the phone, I engaged in a silly ritual I usually perform when I have to make a big decision. I do a self-analysis. I repeat the word "self" three times then I state what the issue is I am confronting. I use this time to weigh pros and cons.

Pros: I walk by faith and not sight. The position would be a challenge. It would be a career step in the right direction, increase in pay. I trust Mr. Nobleman. He has confidence in my ability and I would have his support.

Cons: If I don't pursue this, I may lose out on a really good opportunity. The job is more than one hundred miles from my house. I have only been a director of registration for five months. I would have to manage three facilities.

After talking to my family and a few close friends about the offer, I spent the rest of the day thinking about my decision. The next morning when I woke up, my mind was made up. I made a call to the CFO and told him I was interested in the position. He told me to fill out the application online and someone from Human Resources would follow-up with a interview time and date. The interview was pretty standard nothing really out of the ordinary. I thought I would hear something within a day or so, it turned out to be longer. The HR director called to offer me the position and I accepted. One day driving in to the new job I thought to myself God operates in his own time and when he does it is always worth the wait. I had gone years and years with very little movement in my career and now opportunities abound. This experience reminded of the benefit of exercising patience and waiting on the Lord.

The first month as system director was interesting. I was trying to figure out with my new manager, the Revenue Cycle Director, Ms. Great-N-Wonderful. She talked a mile a minute and never completed a sentence. In addition Mr. Nobleman, the system CFO informed me he was leaving and going back to work at "The Hospital". He stated he was leaving for personal reasons. I wasn't upset with Mr. Nobleman because years earlier I made a similar decision. I was a little perplexed that he didn't share his reservations about staying with "Salvation Hospital" before I accepted the offer. After I got over my mini-pity party, I realized his personal decisions had nothing to do with me. God provided me with this opportunity and I am going to make the most of it. The CFO exited stage left a couple of weeks after our conversation.

After many months, Ms. Sunshine was named CFO. She was a breath of fresh air, full of energy and a woman of faith. I knew God was up to something good. I would go on to work for her almost three years. One day Ms. Sunshine stopped by my office. "Hello Evolving, you have a minute?" I replied, "Of course I do." "Evolving, a colleague is looking for a Revenue Cycle Director. The position sounds like a challenge, it would be a promotion for you and I think it will only be a thirty-five minute commute for you." Over the last two plus years, I drove an hour an twenty minutes to and from work. A thirty-five minute drive would allow me to re-gain an hour and a half back to my day. "Evolving, if you are interested I could forward your information to him. His name is Mr. Do-Little-or-Nothing, he is the CFO of Spirit Hospital." "Absolutely, thank you", I replied. I will e-mail you my resume this evening. A day after our conversation, Ms. Sunshine and I spoke briefly in the hallway. She stated she had forwarded my information to the CFO at Spirit Hospital and I should hear something soon.

Later that day, I received a call from Mr. Do-Little-or-Nothing. Mr. Do-Little stated he had received a copy of my resume and wanted to set up a time to interview me for the Revenue Cycle Director position. During the conversation I asked Mr. Do-Little-or-Nothing if he was looking to hire a manager of patient access also, he said yes. I told him I knew someone who I thought would be a good fit. He asked me to forward him the person's information and told him I would.

Approximately a month before my boss mentioned the revenue cycle position to me, a colleague from "The Hospital" called me. She called to tell me she was looking in the want-ads of the newspaper and she saw an advertisement for two positions, a manager of patient access and a Revenue Cycle Director. My colleague stated, "I have found us new jobs." "What is the name of the hospital?" I asked. "The ad didn't provide that information, the ad simply stated all inquiries should be directed to the Daily News", she replied. As fate would have it, the position Ms. Sunshine told me about and the one my colleague saw in the newspaper were the same positions. My colleague and I were both extended interviews. I don't want to keep you in suspense any longer. We both got the job. Who wouldn't serve a God like that? Not only did he bless me, he used me to bless someone else.

Mom's Messages

1. **When God blesses you, be a blessing to someone else.**
2. **If God has put you in a situation, he will offer his protection and provision.**

Follow The Leader

Matthew 23:12"And whoever exalts himself shall be humbled; and whoever humbles himself shall be exalted. (New American Standard Bible)

Like several of you, as a child I played the game follow the leader. The object of the game was really simple. You emulate what the leader does. As an adult, I find myself taking part in that same exercise; however, now it's not a game. It is real life. The leader is no longer my childhood friend. The leader is Jesus Christ I strive each day to be like and lead like him. I must admit sometimes I strike off in my own direction and he forgives me and allows me to get back in line to receive further direction. My primary goal as a leader is to treat the people in the workplace with the same respect I have for my family and friends.

I was having a conversation with a work associate a while back; she asked me how do I know when I am following God's direction and not my own when I make choices in my career? I replied, you have to align your plan with God's purpose for your life. God has purposed me on this planet to be of service to his people by sharing my time, talents and resources where ever he wants me to go. When he is ready for me to take on another assignment he speaks to my heart, provides the opportunity and I respond accordingly. On occasion, when he speaks and I don't respond to his voice because I have gotten comfortable in a role or not in tune with him like I should be, he allows things to happen to bring me back in line.

Over the years, God has guided me in various directions. There was a stretch in my career where God directed to me accept three different positions at three different facilities within a five year span during one of the nation's worst recessions. Conventional wisdom would have dictated I remain in the first director's role longer, not take a job with more responsibility in another city, stay put until the job market improved.

I have come to accept when God reveals the plan to you, there is no plan B. Evidence of this is shown throughout the bible. In Exodus, God give Moses clear direction on how to lead the people of Israel out of bondage; however the people were disobedient and chose to follow other leaders. As a result the people circled the mountain for forty years until all the non-believers died.

Mom's Messages

1. **Don't discount God –When I graduated from college I read an article somewhere advising the reader to write their desired annual salary on a piece of paper and put it in their purse**

or wallet. It sounded like a good idea at the time I wrote down a number on a small piece of paper and placed it in my wallet. Years later I came across the paper while cleaning out my wallet. To my surprise the number on the paper was about half of what my current salary was. The author of the article stated the purpose of writing a number down was to help the person determine whether they were on track to achieving their maximum salary. The lesson I learned from the exercise as a Christian was to never put a limit on God. I vowed never to anticipate or put barriers on what God can or will do.
2. Always take God at his word!

Dump The Applecart

> Who is wise and understanding among you? By his good conduct let him show his works in the meekness of wisdom. But if you have bitter jealousy and selfish ambition in your hearts, do not boast and be false to truth. This is not the wisdom that comes down from above, but is earthly, unspiritual, demonic. For where jealousy and selfish ambition exist, there will be disorder and every vile practice. (James 3 13 – 16 ESV/3)

Throughout my career I have come in contact with many different attitudes and personalities both good and bad. While it is best to always focus on the good in each situation I would like to share my experiences and the lessons I have learned from my interactions with difficult people. As a manager, I have learned the importance of being in tune with the energy in the department. I have also learned the importance of acting swiftly to address inappropriate behavior. Acting quickly will mitigate or eliminate the problem; in turn, management effectiveness is increased and department goals are met. If you haven't had the distinct experience of dealing with negative people to date, you will at some point in your professional or personal life. For the sake of imagery, I will refer the two types of dominant negative office behaviors as: bruised apples and rotten apples.

A rotten apple may have one or more of following attributes: have an inferiority complex and try to mask it by being mean to fellow co-workers or isolate themselves to small clicks. A rotten apple's biggest fear is being exposed as an insecure and weak person. To say a rotten apple is not disgruntled is like saying oil and water mix. A rotten apple is never content with peace and calm. They see fault in everyone that does not share their point of view. They are often at the center of any confusion in the office. Finally, rotten apples are resistant to change. While helping a rotten apple transition to a good apple is virtually unheard of, we have this assurance that all things are possible with God.

Bruised apples are very delicate individuals they are very easily influenced by their peers. Bruised apples often feel they are overlooked. They spend their entire career living vicariously through other people. In my interactions with "bruised apples", most are perfectly content with spending their work life with the same employer in the same role. Most bruised apples like their jobs; however, they can easily be swayed by those around them. Bruised apples want to be accepted. Unfortunately they are not very discerning in whom they choose to befriend. A 'bruised apple" allowed to remain in an unstable work environment runs an extremely high risk of becoming a rotten apple. In my experience, a rehabilitated bruised apple can be very productive and loyal employees.

My first experiences with a "bruised apple" occurred during my first position in a management role. I was granted the opportunity to supervise the A/R department at "The Local Hospital". The department consisted of fifteen employees. To my surprise, it was an entire department of "bruised apples". On my first day on the job, my boss told me I had two employees whom I should be on the watch for. She went on to say she had done me a favor and had given one of the problem employees a final written warning a week before I arrived. Her final words to me was, "she only needs one more write up and she is out of here". I know those words were meant to comfort me, but I wasn't comforted, I was worried. I had never fired anyone before, as a matter of fact I had never written anyone up before. I sensed I was in for a challenge. To add to the drama, the morale of the department was low. Other departments had a less than amicable relationship with the department and on top of that the employees within the department had a less than amicable relationship with each other.

Week two, I questioned whether I made the right decision. It was a difficult time. I received numerous phone-calls, numerous emails and several visits from other supervisors telling me how bad my employees were. In addition, each employee filed in and out of my office during the two week period briefing me on which of their fellow co-workers were not performing their job, and my boss inquired several times for an update on the employee I was to fire. Work quality and work productivity was low, the trust level among employees towards each other was very bad and the communication between them was virtually non-existent. It was so bad, one employee had created what I called the "great wall" around her cube, there was about twenty boxes stacked on top of each other. The boxes were put there to ward off evil spirits. Actually the employee stated the boxes we around her cube so she wouldn't have to interact with anyone. Employees came into work day in and day out and didn't offer a good morning when they arrived or a good evening when the left. If I was going to be successful in this role, I knew I had to do something immediately. The problem was I didn't have a clue what to do.

Week Three, after reflecting over the weekend and being rejuvenated from Sunday's sermon I approached the week with a renewed sense of optimism and a resolve that everything would work out. I arrived to the office very early. The first task on my list of things to do for the day, tear down the Great wall, literally and figuratively. The employee who worked behind the wall of boxes came in shortly after I did. I waited until she got settled. I went to her desk and asked her to come to my office. "Good morning Under-the-Radar, will you come to my office?" Under-the-Radar replied, "Sure, I will be there in a minute." A few moments later

Under-the-Radar arrived to my office. "Have a seat Under-the-Radar." You have been in the department for years; I think you have a great deal of knowledge and insights and are valuable to the department. I would like to hear any suggestions you may have on how we could make improvements in the department." Under-the-Radar paused a few minutes before responding to my question. To my surprise, this very shy and timid person opened up and shared her ideas on everything from work flow to employee morale and communications with other departments. "Under-the-Radar thank you so much for sharing, you have some really great ideas and your insights are very valuable." I thanked her for suggestions, I told her I wanted to talk about the boxes. I told her the department was changing and I needed her help. I suggested a good first step toward changing the image of the department would be to take the boxes down. I knew she was uncomfortable with my suggestion but she agreed.

Shortly after my conversation with this employee, the rest of employees started to arrive for the day. I walked out in the area, spoke to everyone and asked them to go to the conference room for a quick staff meeting. On my way to the conference room, I stopped by Under-the-Radar's desk to help her take the boxes down. After taking care of that, Under-the-Radar and I headed to the conference room. Over the next few months, I saw productivity increased, morale increased and over the next year I saw friendships formed, relationships with other departments were mended and employees from other department were constantly asking to transfer to the department.

Mom's Messages

1. **Listen, care, compliment**
2. **Set the table and folks will sit down to eat.**
3. **If people trust you, they will follow you.**

Be Still And Know

Matthew 6:33-34 New International Version (NIV)
³³ But seek first his kingdom and his righteousness, and all these things will be given to you as well. ³⁴ Therefore do not worry about tomorrow, for tomorrow will worry about itself. Each day has enough trouble of its own.

Five years ago I experienced a profound spiritual experience. I was the new Patient Access Director for a three hospital system. My boss, Ms. Great-N-Wonderful was a very high strung, bright, out spoken young lady. She had the potential to be a great leader but unfortunately she stood in her own way. Early on I knew there would be tension between Ms. Great-N-wonderful and myself. I was hired into the position under the advisement of the hospital's CFO, Mr. Nobleman. Mr. Nobleman was the CFO at my former employer. I really think Ms. Great-N-Wonderful resented being heavily encouraged to hire me.

My first month on the job, Ms. Great-N-Wonderful was very helpful, she gave me one on one attention and allowed me to accompany her to meetings, she showed me how to log on and maneuver around the computer system. She welcomed me with open arms. I thought at the time at least. Unfortunately, the honeymoon was short lived. I arrived to work one morning, there was a voice message on my office phone. The message was from the CFO. The message stated: "Good morning Evolving, this is Mr. Nobleman, please come see me when you get in". I was a little startled receiving a message like that from the CFO first thing in the morning; it didn't make me feel warm and fuzzy. I thought to myself, "Why does he want to see me, I haven't been here long enough to mess anything up?" I quickly made my way over to Mr. Nobleman's office, he was there seated behind the desk. "Good morning Mr. Nobleman, you wanted to see me?" "Yes Evolving come on in. I wanted to let you know Friday will be my last day here I am going to go back to "The Hospital". I took a moment to gather my thoughts then spoke, "Mr. Nobleman is the hospital in financial trouble or something?" "No, I am leaving for personal reasons", he replied. I asked Mr. Nobleman what would happen to my job. I figured this was an appropriate question to ask considering Mr. Nobleman recruited me for the position. He replied, "Your job will not be affected, you will be fine." I extended my hand to Mr. Nobleman, wished him well and thanked him for everything he had done for me. "Don't mention it", he replied. I went back to my office and attempted to get my work day started.

As I was waiting for the computer to boot up, I hear a knock on the door. It was Ms. Great-N-wonderful. "Good morning I guess you heard your boy leaving", Ms. Great-N-Wonderful stated. "Yes, I heard Mr. Nobleman is leaving and he is not my boy", I replied. "You know what I mean, he is the reason you bought your butt down here", she replied. "I am here because Mr. Nobleman knows my work and because I am qualified". After a few moments of trading comments, Ms. Great-N-wonderful she said "I don't know what's going to happen to your job." "What do you mean", I replied? "These folks down here are something else, they may think your position is not needed", Ms. Great-N-Wonderful stated. "I am not worried, you are my boss and if anyone thinks anything about me it would be based on your comments." I could tell immediately my comments set off a five-alarm fire inside Ms. Great-N-Wonderful. Her eyes seemed to double in size, he nostrils flared and her face became flushed. "I don't know who you think you talking to. If your job is eliminated, it won't have anything to do with me", she replied. "Ms. Great-N-Wonderful I apologize if I offended you, what I meant to say was you are the person who can speak to the matter of whether my position is needed." Ms. Great-N-Wonderful replied, "I can tell them your position is needed but they are not going to listen to me, they will go by what they see." From the way the conversation was going, it was time for Ms. Great-N-Wonderful or me to step up and act like the grown up in the room. It seemed she was content playing the role of a ten year old bully so I assumed the adult role. "I am not going to worry Ms. Great-N-Wonderful things will work out just fine." She replied, "I hope so, anyway I got a meeting to go to. I will talk to you later." She replied and exited the room.

On the way home that afternoon, my phone rung it was Ms. Great-N-Wonderful. I answered the call, "Hello". "Hey Evolving, this is Ms. Great-N-Wonderful. Have you thought anymore about the conversation we had this morning?" "No", I replied. Ms. Great-N-Wonderful began to offer me some advice, "if I were you, I would call Mr. Nobleman and ask him for my old job back." I replied, "There is no old job, my old position was filled with an internal candidate and besides the position I have now was a big promotion for me", I replied. Ms. Great-N-Wonderful replied "I am only trying to help you. He should be able to find you something there since he is the one who decided to bring you here." I replied, "I am good where I am, I am not leaving." I could hear the frustration in her voice that was not the response she was seeking. I could hear one of her children in the background trying to get her attention. "I am coming", she replied. "Evolving, I got to go help my child with homework I will see you tomorrow." "Good night Ms. Great-N-Wonderful, I will see you tomorrow. For the next couple of weeks, I would receive an evening call from my boss encouraging me to seek a position with my former employer. Each time I would tell her I was not leaving. I think Ms. Great-N-Wonderful finally figured out I was not going to leave by her asking me so she changed her strategy.

A week or so after the last phone call from my boss, I noticed Ms. Great-N-Wonderful was interacting with me less and less. I was not one to easily accept the brushoff, so I started to communicate with her almost exclusively by e-mail even when she would call me on the phone I would follow-up with an e-mail summarizing the conversation. Ms. Great-N-Wonderful being a smart lady realized I was creating a paper trail so she would respond to my questions in a timely fashion. In addition to the cold shoulder, Ms. Great-N-Wonderful stopped inviting me to meetings concerning my area of responsibility. She gave me menial tasks to perform and would often try to embarrass me in front of my peers during staff meetings. On a typical work day I would spend most of the day surfing the internet about industry best practices, ESPN or some news sites, go to lunch for an hour, come back to my office and pick up where I left off. I found myself quickly getting bored and frustrated with my daily routine. My first thought was to go to the system CEO to complain. Realizing I was the new kid on the block and no one knew who I was or what I did I dismissed this option. Although I prayed for an answer, I thought God was ignoring me because it appeared that my situation wasn't changing for the better or so I thought.

At the time I was in graduate school, I was staying up late each night trying to complete my homework assignments. I decided instead of me be bored and unproductive by surfing the internet at work I could bring my books to work and study. Each day I would come to work, close my office door and study this routine lasted over six months.

Eventually the hospital hired the Interim CFO, Ms. Sunshine and thankfully God let her find favor in me. Ms. Sunshine and I met casually. I didn't know what position she held when we met. To me, she was a nice lady that worked in the building. We would greet each or with a "Happy whatever day it was" as we passed in the hallway. From time to time, she would ask how things were going between Ms. Great-N-Wonderful and me. I would respond, ok.

One day Ms. Sunshine came to my office to ask if I would like to work for her. Before she told me what the job was I said "yes". She went on to tell me my title and job responsibilities would change but my salary and hours would be the same. Ms. Sunshine told me I would start my new role at the beginning of the next pay period. I thanked Ms. Sunshine for the opportunity. "You are welcome, by the way I will share the news with Ms. Great-N-Wonderful" she replied as she exited the office. I was elated I couldn't stop smiling the rest of the day.

Early the next day Ms. Great-N-Wonderful visited me. She stopped by to inform me Ms. Sunshine told her I would no longer be her employee in less than two weeks. "Evolving, why didn't you tell me you were going to work for Ms. Sunshine?" "Ms. Great-N-Wonderful" it was not my place to make to share that information with you. Ms. Sunshine is your superior it is her right to share that information with you." "This is how you do me, I treated you good', she replied. I sat quietly. Ms. Great-N-Wonderful gave me a really nasty look; she then turned around and walked away. I thought because God didn't reveal a plan of action for me to take or give me words to say he wasn't going to answer my prayer. On the contrary, he answered my prayer. God was telling me to do nothing he would take care of everything and he did. Amen…

Mom's Messages

1. **Humble yourself and let God work.**
2. **God created the heavens, earth and you. He doesn't need your help.**
3. **Stop trying to tend to God's business. Let God be God.**

Carpooling With The Devil

King James Version of <u>Joshua 1:8</u>.

This book of the law shall not depart out of thy mouth; but thou shalt meditate therein day and night, that thou mayest observe to do according to all that is written therein: for then thou shalt make thy way prosperous, and then thou shalt have good success.

I have heard countless people: parents, physicians, dieticians, media personalities and scientists emphasize the importance of eating a well-balanced breakfast each morning. However, few have echoed those sentiments in regards to feeding your spiritual self each morning through mediation, reading or simply setting aside time to think good thoughts. I submit feeding the spiritual self is equally important. The devil is always waiting for an opportunity to exploit our weaknesses and ultimately uses those weaknesses as a weapon to destroy us. We must always be aware of his presence and take measures to guard against his attacks.

I was on the freeway heading to work one morning; I saw a car in the rear view mirror approaching at an extremely fast speed. I attempted to get in the slow lane to allow the driver to pass, but couldn't because of oncoming traffic. I could quickly see the driver wasn't happy with me; he began to follow closely behind me in an attempt to get me out of his way. My heart rate increased, my palms were sweaty. I increased my speed in hopes of merging to the slow lane. Finally I see a break in traffic; I merge over to the slow lane. At that moment I took a deep sigh of relief, "I am glad that crazy man is gone". He must have heard me call him out of his name because a few moments later, the driver abruptly swerved out the fast lane into my lane. Once he got in front of me, he slowed down. I was becoming angry. I thought, "Why is this guy acting a fool this morning? Someone could get hurt." I waited for my opportunity and merged back into the fast lane. The driver decides to get in the fast lane as well. The driver slowed up briefly then sped off. At that moment my first thought was to catch up with him and cut him off. Without notice or invitation, the devil invited himself into my car. I could hear him saying "I know you are not going to let that idiot get away with cutting in front of you. Blow your horn, do something. Better yet let me drive." I resisted the devil's plea. I reduced my speed, turned on the radio and continued my commute to work.

Although I was able to put my emotions in check, the tone for my day was set. I found myself being agitated all day. The small things that I would normally overlook like someone walking in the building before me and letting the door shut behind them, people entering the room and not speaking, everything rubbed me the wrong way. Not only did my negative mindset affect my day, it also directly or indirectly affected those around me. I found myself being less social and more direct with my employees. I was careful not to be rude, but I certainly was not my usual chipper self. One of my employees asked me was everything okay. "It's been a long day, but I am good." "I knew something was wrong with you, you don't seem like yourself today." "Really, I am good. How are you doing today?" "Fine", she replied. I wished her a good rest of the day and headed back to work.

The devil is reactive, his thoughts aren't original. He is the ultimate agitator. His role is to convince you that your un-holy thoughts should be acted on. His plan is always the same, to cause conflict and destruction. Once we invite him in, he hangs around until his mission is accomplished. We must be mindful of the devil's tricks and arm ourselves with tools to defeat him. Recognize his work; guard your thoughts by praying, reading the word of God and inundating your psyche with good thoughts.

Mom's Messages

1. **Ward off the devil by creating a plan of your own, he doesn't like hand to hand combat.**
2. **Cleansing your mind each day opens a pathway to the place within you where God resides.**
3. **Don't invite strangers into your car.**

Morning Prayer

Thank you Jesus for interceding on my behalf, I thank you for every mercy you have extended towards me. Father I ask you to keep my mind on you and your ways. Let my interactions with your people be a reflection of the love, patience and understanding you have shown towards me. Amen

The $800,000 Meeting

Psalm 37:1-4 New International Version (NIV)
[1] Do not fret because of those who are evil or be envious of those who do wrong; [2] for like the grass they will soon wither, like green plants they will soon die away. [3] Trust in the Lord and do good; dwell in the land and enjoy safe pasture. [4] Take delight in the Lord, and he will give you the desires of your heart

My boss Mr. Middle -of-the-Road appears in the doorway of my cube "Good morning Evolving, Motivation wants to see us in her office." "Good morning, I will be right there." I took a moment to contemplate what could she possibly want this time. My director, Motivation is definitely not the president of the Evolving fan club so I anticipate this isn't an invitation to a love feast. I gathered a note pad and pencil, headed down the long corridor to Motivation's office. As I walked down the long corridor, memories of past visits to her office flooded my mind. I thought about the time, I'd just returned to the office from vacation. Motivation summoned me to her office where she berated me for almost thirty minutes. I arrived at Motivation's office, peeked in her doorway and there she was seated around the conference table with my boss, Mr. Middle-of-the-Road and the senior accountant. I entered the office and greeted everyone, "Good morning". "Good morning" replied the senior accountant, Mr. Middle-of-the-Road and Motivation didn't respond. I pulled the chair out from the table and took a seat. At this point my hands are sweating and my deodorant is working overtime. I am nervous for the following reasons: the cold reception I received, the dead silence in the room, Motivation sitting directly across from me with this intimidating look on her face, and no one has stated why I was called into the meeting.

"Do you know why you are here?" "I couldn't imagine why Motivation." "You are here because you made an $800,000 journal entry during the end of month close out process. The entry you made resulted in the hospital's books being overstated by $800,000." I took a deep breath before I replied. "Excuse me; you said I made an $800,000 entry? "Yes, Motivation replied. "May I see the journal entry you are speaking of?" Motivation's tone immediately changed, she began to speak in a very defensive manner. "You don't need to see the entry, we are trying to help you all you need to do is sign this document." Motivation picked up the document in front of her, gave it to Mr. Middle- of-the -Road and he passed it to me. It was a disciplinary action stating I acknowledge and accept responsibility for the error I was being accused of committing.

As I read over the document, I look up every now and then to see the expressions on everyone's face. Mr. Middle-of-the-Road is expressionless as usual, the senior accountant is looking puzzled and Motivation face has turned red with anger. After reading over the document, I asked for a copy of the journal entry. "You will not see a copy of the entry", Motivation replied. I replied, "If you can't provide me with a copy of the error, I am not going to sign this form." At this point of the conversation, diplomacy and common sense left the room. "You will not see a copy of the entry" Motivation repeated. I felt myself getting anxious so I took a couple of deep breaths, adjusted my tie, composed my thoughts and replied "I don't need to see a copy of the error because I am a junior accountant and if an error of that magnitude was allowed to be processed you and the other members around the table are responsible for the error not me." The senior accountant replied "I am not your boss; I am not responsible for your work." I turn my attention to Mr. Middle of the Road. "Mr. Middle-of-the-Road, aren't you, the senior accountant and Motivation responsible for reviewing and approving all journal entries before they are finalized?" Yes, he replied. After my boss replied, I asked Motivation if there wasn't anything else to discuss may I be excused back to work. "You can leave", she replied. Before leaving I picked up the unsigned document handed it to my boss and exited the office.

I returned to my office realizing Motivation was up to something bad and she may have failed this time but there will be other times. I resolved from that moment to make sure I cross every T and dot every I. Anytime I communicated with Motivation or Mr.

Middle-of-the-Road regarding work I would send each of them a follow-up e-mail recapping my take on the conversation. If there was an inkling of uncertainty about what actions or directions I should take on an account I would seek advice from a member of the leadership team.

Later during the day, I went to the senior accountant's office to let him know I wasn't blaming him for what happened. He told me no harm was done. "I am glad to hear that. ", I replied. I changed the subject and we spent a few moments engaging in conversation about the stock market. The senior accountant was heavy into day trading. Changing the subject from the incident that happened earlier to something he enjoyed completely change the mood in the room.

After my conversation with the senior accountant, I went next door to Mr. Middle-of-the-Road's office. "Do you have a minute?" "Sure Evolving, come in." "I want to talk to you about the conversation we had in Motivation's office this morning." "What would you like to know?" "Sir, why did we have to meet in her office? In times pass, you would bring me to your office or come to my office if there was a question about an action I took." "Well, Well, Motivation called the meeting because of the magnitude of the error. She said we needed to write you up." The more Mr. Middle-of-the-Road spoke the more I realized something more than what he was revealing was going on. I concluded my conversation with Mr. Middle -of –the-Road, thanked him for his time and headed back to work.

Mom's Messages

1. **The truth is the only evidence you will need.**
2. **Try to remain calm; you don't have to defend the truth.**
3. **Think before you speak.**

You Are Not The Boss Of Me

[10] Finally, be strong in the Lord and in his mighty power. [11] Put on the full armor of God, so that you can take your stand against the devil's schemes. [12] For our struggle is not against flesh and blood, but against the rulers, against the authorities, against the powers of this dark world and against the spiritual forces of evil in the heavenly realms. [13] Therefore put on the full armor of God, so that when the day of evil comes, you may be able to stand your ground, and after you have done everything, to stand. [14] Stand firm then, with the belt of truth buckled around your waist, with the breastplate of righteousness in place, [15] and with your feet fitted with the readiness that comes from the gospel of peace. [16] In addition to all this, take up the shield of faith, with which you can extinguish all the flaming arrows of the evil one. [17] Take the helmet of salvation and the sword of the Spirit, which is the word of God. Ephesians 6:10-17 New International Version (NIV)

Managing people is not an easy task. Many days I have left the office scratching my head wondering why some people are determined to be difficult and uncooperative despite my efforts to ensure they were encouraged by me, provided the necessary tools and resources to aid them in being productive and engaged employees. In my career I have experienced some difficult people but none more difficult and disrespectful than Turmoil and Strife. They thumbed their noses at management, disregarded the chain of command, and resisted change at every turn. These two ladies tested my patience, made me try harder, pray more and trust God implicitly.

Strife was a bitter woman, she offered me nothing but disdain and disrespect from day one. Like Misery-Loves-Company, Strife was demoted prior to me coming on board at the hospital. I can re-call one occasion, Turmoil and Strife's manager, Ms. Nice-Nasty and I provided lunch for the staff, Strife was overheard telling her fellow co-workers she fed her free meal to the dogs. She went to HR to complain on me and her manager at least twice a month. Turmoil was a little more subtle but just as devious. She was a long-term employee with entitlement issues. She thought she should be promoted based on years of service not job knowledge and professionalism. During my time at Spirit Hospital, Turmoil applied for eight or nine different positions. Turmoil also went to HR on numerous occasions, each time it was based on an issue Strife has complained about previously.

Week Two at Spirit Hospital - I was conducting my morning rounds through the six areas that fall under my leadership. As I approached one of the areas, I saw patients standing around the walls, all of the chairs in the lobby were occupied but the staff didn't seem bothered by the crowd or the comments being made by the restless patients and their families. In fact I overheard Turmoil, tell a patient" Mam we so slow because management let the greeter go and the computers are so slow, we going as fast as we can." Turmoil was correct to a degree, the computers could stand a memory upgrade; however, Turmoil and the other clerks added to the problem. The ladies seem to have very little concern for patient satisfaction. I walked around the desk to use the phone.

I called the manager of the area to come over to assist with the crowd. Strife, the shift lead was standing in the walk way. I asked Strife, why didn't she call her manager for help? "I was too busy to call", she replied. I could see my questioning the staff wasn't going to get the line moving any faster so I changed my strategy. I rolled up my sleeves to help. I picked up the sign-in sheet and started distributing patient labels to the clerks as they finished registering a patient. Strife had just completed a registration. I extend my hand towards Strife to hand her the label for her next patient. Strife doesn't acknowledge my presence. I walk closer to her and say "Strife here is the label for the next patient." Strife replies" I am going on break."

"Strife, do you see all of the patients in the lobby and around the walls waiting to be registered? Many of these people haven't eaten for hours some are really sick. Do you think it is ok for them to continue to wait while you go to break?" Strife replied "I have been here for hours. I am going to take a break". "Strife, lunches are the only breaks you are entitled to per the law. Other breaks are only allowed if your workload permits." Strife gives me the dreadful just die look. In the meantime patients are starting to notice the conversation between Strife and myself. I was trying to remain calm and professional but Strife is pushing all the wrong buttons. Just when I thought the situation couldn't get any worse, Strife snatches the label from my hand. It seems the room went dark for 30 seconds. In all of my years working, no one had ever done such an ugly thing to me. I paused for a moment before responding, I didn't want to draw more attention to the situation but I had to address her behavior. "Strife yours actions were inappropriate and unacceptable." Strife began to manufacture tears. Strife's manager had arrived in the area. She walked over to Strife. "Strife what is wrong?" Strife replied "He told me I couldn't go to the restroom." "I never said such a thing, Strife was told she couldn't take a break until the crowd was taken care of she didn't not mention the restroom." Strife really starts to bring on the tears. Strife tells her manager she is going to resign. I step away from the situation and continue helping the other ladies register patients.

Later on during the day, I receive an e-mail from the Director of Human Resources. The HR director forwarded an e-mail he received from Strife. In the e-mail, Strife stated she was going to resign from her position. I immediately called the director of HR to tell him the manager and I would accept her resignation. The director replied "She needs her job, talk to her and give her a verbal warning." I was surprised at his response.

In past positions, HR is always ready to let troubled employees go. I would later learn HR and Strife had a very good relationship. In my two years and nine months at Spirit Hospital, Strife never addressed any of her complaints or concerns with me or her manager. Strife had a direct line to HR, her and Turmoil were exceptions to the chain of command policy; they were allowed to have their concerns addressed by HR and not management. I spoke with my boss, Mr. Do-little-or-Nothing about this and he stated the ladies had a right to go straight to HR. On numerous occasions I asked the HR director to set up a conference with Turmoil in his office, each time he ignored my request.

In addition to the incident above, Strife lodged numerous complaints and sent numerous e-mails to HR regarding her manager and me. Strife not only sent her personal complaints she sent e-mails on behalf of other employees in the area. Strife was so disrespectful and defiant in fact her job description had to be re-written to include a line stating she would refer to me by my name. Strife had this horrible habit of referring to me as him or he in my presence and she never looked me in the eyes when speaking to her.

Not to be out done by Strife, Turmoil was a force to reckon with. Turmoil was a born follower; unfortunately, her leader was Strife. Turmoil also lodged numerous complaints against her manager and me. One day I was in the area helping the staff register patients. I walked over to hand Turmoil the sticker of her next patient. "Turmoil, here is your next patient." Turmoil replies, "Give it to him." She was referring to a fellow co-worker who was waiting on a patient. "Here is your next patient", I responded. Turmoil reluctantly takes the label and calls the patient to her desk to register them. After Turmoil completed the registration, I walked over to address her previous comment. I didn't want to discipline Turmoil in front of her co-workers so I told her to meet me in her manager's office the next morning at the beginning of her shift.

Turmoil reported to her manager's office at the requested time. Her manager and I were already seated. "Good morning sir and mam." "Good morning" the manager and I replied. "Turmoil, you were asked to meet us here today to discuss your behavior on yesterday afternoon." "Yes sir" Turmoil replied. "Turmoil, I am the director of the department. I am your manager's superior. Do you understand the chain of command?" "Yes" Turmoil replied. "Your behavior on yesterday was deplorable, I should have written you up on the spot but I didn't want to embarrass you in front of the customers and your fellow co-workers." Turmoil replied, "Sir I won't ever do that again. I apologize." I told Turmoil this counseling would serve as a verbal warning for her conduct. Turmoil said she understood. "Turmoil any further displays of insubordination would lead to additional disciplinary action up to and including termination." "I understand sir", Turmoil replied. "Turmoil you may be excused; have a good day." "You too sir and mam", Turmoil replied.

After the counseling with Turmoil, she never refused or questioned a request from her manager or me. Unfortunately, Turmoil continued to provide mediocre service to our patients and her disposition was far less than sunny. Turmoil was far more concerned with being off work and the replacing the greeter position that was eliminated almost four years prior. She continued to go to HR to complain on Ms. Nice-Nasty and me.

Mom's Messages

1. **Meet people where they are because only God can heal a broken person.**
2. **Admonish bad behavior every time.**
3. **Acknowledge your boundaries.**
4. **A fire left unattended in the forest, puts the whole forest in jeopardy of burning down.**

All In A Day's Work...

Proverbs 15:18 New International Version (NIV)
[18] A hot-tempered person stirs up conflict,
but the one who is patient calms a quarrel.

People never cease to amaze me. I thought to myself as Mad-for-no- Reason, one of my employees exited my office. I invited him into my office to review his ninety day evaluation. I carefully went over each evaluation category with Mad-for-no-Reason and asked if he had comments. "I don't have anything to add" he replied. Up to this point the evaluation was going along smoothly. After reviewing all the categories, I told Mad-for-no-Reason he had satisfactorily completed his probationary period and officially welcomed him to the team. He smiled after hearing the news. "Do you have any questions for me?" "Yes" he replied. "When will I get my raise and how much will it be?" "Mad-for-no-Reason, why do you think you should receive a raise after ninety days?" "I did my job", he replied. "Yes you did and you were paid for the job you performed", I replied. "Did you learn any of your fellow co-workers jobs during your ninety days?" Mad-for-no-Reason had a puzzled look on his face. "No", he replied. "Mad-for-no-Reason did you learn and perform my job during your ninety day probationary period?" "No" he replied.

"Mad-for-no-Reason look at this job as an opportunity to increase your skill set. Learn as much as you can and the opportunity to earn more will come." From the expression on Mad-for-no-Reason' face he wasn't feeling my response but he shook his head to confirm he understood.

In future months, I would learn Mad-for-no-Reason really didn't understand the talk we had. He became bitter and began to share his dissatisfaction with his co-workers. Mad-for-no-Reason' performance decreased as well. I felt it was time to have another discussion with Mad-for-no-Reason. All in all, Mad-for-no-Reason was a good employee and more importantly he had great potential. I knew a second talk would help but I knew I had to be more assertive in my tone this time. I spent an hour or two trying to determine the approach I would take.

I called Mad-for-no-Reason in my office fifteen minutes before his shift ended. Mad-for-no-Reason came into my office and took a seat. "Mad-for-no-Reason, I was walking through the office and overheard your conversation with a co-worker regarding your pay. During your ninety day evaluation you told me you understood my explanation regarding a pay raise." Mad-for-no-Reason shoulders began to tense up. "Mad-for-no-Reason, I took the liberty and pulled your application, per your application you were making $7 per hour at your previous job and you are currently making $10 per hour. I think your time would be better spent on doing the job you were hired to do, learn other skills or find you another job, I am not going to allow you to spread negativity throughout the office." Mad-for-no-Reason promised he would stop complaining and focus more on doing a good job. I shook his hand and told him to enjoy the rest of the day. Mad-for-no-Reason' attitude did improve dramatically after the conversation and we never had to have another conversation about his pay again.

Mom's Messages

1. **People may not get the point the first time, go over it again.**
2. **Allow a person to tell their story.**
3. **Don't let anger be your first response.**

Fair Is Fair??

Proverbs 19:11 New International Version (NIV)
¹¹ A person's wisdom yields patience; it is to one's glory to overlook an offense.

Throughout my career I have tried very hard to do three things. First, make each department or division I am responsible for more effective and efficient. Second, be an encouraging leader. Third, be fair. One day without warning, one of my employees confronted me regarding my fairness towards her. I was definitely taken back by her statement but I found the conversation helpful.

A knock on the door got my attention; I looked up from my computer to see who it was. It was Plain-N-Simple. Plain-N-Simple was one the most productive and pleasant employees I had. Plain-N-Simple was always on time, worked independently and always willing to help when called upon. From the look on Plain-N-Simple's face, I could tell something was bothering her. I invited Plain-N-Simple in and ask her if there was something I could do for her. "Yes" Plain-N-Simple replied. "I need to talk to you about something." "Not a problem", I replied. Please close the door and have a seat." She took a seat and sat there for a moment as if she was searching for the right words to say. After a minute or two Plain-N-Simple spoke, "I don't think you are treating me fairly, you allow the other employees to goof off, you don't hold them accountable like you do me. I have to take up their slack all the time." I waited until Plain-N-Simple completed her comments and then I spoke. "Plain-N-Simple, have any of your requests for time off been denied?" "No" she replied. "Have you ever been denied the opportunity to leave early when your child was sick?" "No", Plain-N-Simple replied. "Whenever you have asked for overtime, didn't I approve it?" "Yes" "Plain-N-Simple didn't you receive an above average raise and an excellent evaluation last year?" Again Plain-N-Simple replied yes. I then felt it was necessary to probe further. I asked Plain-N-Simple the following questions: "Do you know if any of the employees you consider goofing off have received disciplinary action? Do you know if they received a merit raise or good evaluations last year?" "No", Plain-N-Simple replied.

I told Plain-N-Simple I was concerned that her visit was more about how her co-workers were being treated than her treatment. Plain-N-Simple began to sob uncontrollably. I offered her a tissue and followed up with another question. "Plain-N-Simple, how would you feel if I opened the door to my office and allowed the other employees to witness you crying?" "I wouldn't like it" she replied. Plain-N-Simple apologized for accusing me of not being fair. I accepted her apology and allowed her to regain her composure before returning back to work. "Plain-N-Simple anytime you have issues or concerns feel free to come see me, thank you for feeling comfortable enough to share your thoughts with me."

Whenever I am confronted with making a decision regarding the treatment of an employee, I reflect on the conversation I had with Plain-N-Simple many years ago. My conversation with her helped me realize perception can be so very different from the intentions of the person making the decision. My rule concerning fairness is: Base your actions on what is right and not on the party or parties involved.

Mom's Messages

1. **Fairness is applying the same deference to a situation regardless of the parties involved.**
2. **Humility is the cornerstone of fairness.**

Sometimes You Got To Beat A Dead Horse

Proverbs 24:16 New International Version (NIV)
[16] for though the righteous fall seven times, they rise again, but the wicked stumble when calamity strikes.

One day after work I visited the hospital's website to see if there were any positions I was interested in and qualified for. I didn't see any vacant positions that matched my qualifications. While on the website I noticed the hospital posted various job classes and the salary ranges for each class. I searched to find my job class on the list. To my surprise the base salary listed for my position was approximately $3,000 greater than my current salary. I quickly wrote down the information and the following day went to my supervisor, Mr. Middle-of-the-Road to discuss the information I discovered the night before. I knocked on the door before entering. "Mr. Middle of the Road, do you have a moment?" "Sure, come on in." "Sir I was online last night and I noticed the base salary posted for my position on the hospital's website is $3,000 more than my current salary." "Are you sure", he replied. "I am sure. Would you like me to pull up the information on your computer?" Mr. Middle of the Road said that wouldn't be necessary. "Sir, what steps do I need to take to correct this mistake?" "Evolving I will talk with Motivation to find out what should be done." "Thank you sir, when should I follow up with you regarding this issue?" "Check back with me in two days", he replied.

A couple of days later, I stopped by Mr. Middle-of-the-Road's office to find out if he had any news regarding my salary. As I was about to knock on Mr. Middle of the Road's office door and he looked up from his computer. "Evolving, I was going to come by to see you later. I spoke with Motivation and she said you are not entitled to a salary adjustment." "Sir I have been here almost four years, are you telling me it is ok for me to make $3,000 less than a person off the street with no experience. This is not fair sir. I am going to follow up with Motivation." Mr. Middle-of-the-Road responded "Evolving she is not going to budge on this, you are beating a dead horse."

I went straight to Motivation's office. I think Mr. Middle-of-the-Road must have given Motivation a heads up because when I arrived at her office she met me at her doorway. "Do you have a moment", I asked? "Just a moment, I am leaving for a meeting", she replied. "I spoke with Mr. Middle-of-the-Road a couple of days ago regarding my salary and today he told me there was no chance my salary would be adjusted." Motivation replied, "Your supervisor did bring this issue to my attention and I told him there was no need to adjust your pay." "How is that possible? I am making $3,000 less than the base salary for my position." Motivation walked away while I was talking. Half-way down the hall she responded, "As I stated, I am on the way to a meeting. Your salary will not be adjusted."

I stood there in the hallway with my mouth open as Motivation walked away, I contemplated my next move. I went back to my office to gather my thoughts. After an hour or so, I decided to call the Director of compensation. After giving the director a brief summary of my complaint, she agreed to meet with me.

The meeting was held in the director's office approximately two days after the phone call. "Good morning Ms. Doing-My-Job, thanks for taking time to meet with me." "Good morning, not a problem, she replied." "Evolving, after our conversation I reviewed the salary range for your position and reviewed your current salary, you are correct your current salary doesn't reflect your experience and you shouldn't make less than the base of the salary range." "I will be able to help you, but you will have to discuss your issue with Motivation's boss, he will have to give his approval." I thanked Ms. Doing-My-Job for her advice and assured her I would set up a meeting with Motivation's boss.

I left Ms. Doing-My-Job's office feeling semi-relieved, but was mindful that another hurdle awaited me. Motivation's boss was the CFO of the hospital and I didn't think he would want to spend his time meeting with a complaining staff accountant. As I was heading down the street back to my office, I convinced myself to stop by the CFO's office to set up a meeting with his secretary. To my surprise, the secretary told me Mr.

Call-it-like-I-see-it was in his office; she told me to have a seat and she would see if he was available to speak with me. "Evolving, Mr. Call-it-like-I-see-it can see you now." I didn't have time to be nervous, this was my moment and I can't blow it. I entered Mr. Call-it's office. He stood up from his chair to meet me. Mr. Call-it was a very imposing individual he was approximately 6'4" and approximately 300 pounds. "Evolving, what can I do for you?" "Sir, Ms. Doing-My-Job suggested I speak with you regarding a problem we discovered with my salary. Sir, I brought this issue to my supervisor and his supervisor's attention and both told me my they were going to look into the issue." Mr. Call-it-like-I-see-it responded "Evolving you don't need to worry about this anymore. If you are due a salary adjustment, we will make this right." I thanked Mr. Call-it for his time.

Mr. Call-it-like-I-see-it was true to his word. A week after my meeting with him, I received a call from the Director of Compensation. During the call she informed me I would be receiving an adjustment to my annual salary of $3,000 and I would also be receiving retro-active pay back to the date of the range change. I thanked Ms. Doing-my-Job for her help. After I hung up the phone, I recall taking a deep sigh and thanking God everything worked out in this situation.

Mom's Messages

1. God is working on your behalf.
2. Perseverance is a strong tool when used constructively.
3. Persistence is like a boxing match, be prepared to go 12 rounds.

Escape To Paradise

Philippians 4:11-13New International Version (NIV)
¹¹ I am not saying this because I am in need, for I have learned to be content whatever the circumstances.
¹² I know what it is to be in need, and I know what it is to have plenty. I have learned the secret of being content in any and every situation, whether well fed or hungry, whether living in plenty or in want. ¹³ I can do all this through him who gives me strength.

While working at Major General Hospital was a suffocating type of experience most days, there were those rare moments when I felt free and content. The old adage when you have lemons make lemon aide applies here. Day after day I came into work wondering what land mines Motivation had set for me. She was never one to disappoint. I recall on one occasion, she added additional duties to my daily responsibilities. The new duties had nothing to do with my position. I wondered; how does she keep getting away with doing bad things? Years later I realized she wasn't getting away with anything. In each situation, God allowed those things to happen so I could lean and trust on him.

Mr. Middle-of-the-Road and I were about to complete our bi-weekly one-on-one meeting. "Evolving, there is one other thing I would like to discuss before we conclude. Motivation, asked that I tell you beginning

Monday you will be responsible for delivering and picking up the mail for the department." "You have to be kidding me Mr. Middle-of-the-Road we have a courier that does that. I was hired to work here as an accountant not a courier." He replied, "The courier only comes once a day, you will be picking up and delivering those things that come up after the courier has made his daily run. Evolving I understand your frustration, it won't be that bad."

Mr. Middle-of-the-Road was actually correct. After my first week, I actually looked forward to the making the daily pick up and deliveries. My new responsibility allowed me to get out the office an hour each day. I met people throughout the hospital I didn't have the opportunity to meet before now. I actually met my mentor, A-matter-of-Fact on my mail run one day. I had to deliver something to her. We began a conversation and have been connected since then. In addition to enlarging my network, this new responsibility allowed me to slow down to appreciate and observe what God was doing in my life. While walking down the street with the mail, I would pay attention to the blueness of the sky, listen actively to the sounds of people and cars passing by. I enjoyed feeling the warmth of the sun's rays on my face.

One day I was walking to a building on campus to pick up a package for my boss. I heard someone yelling from behind me. I stopped to see who it was. It was a guy whom I did not know. From the way he was dressed and looked, he appeared to be homeless. "Hey brother, you mighty clean with your Brooks Brothers' suit and your shiny shoes on. I bet you got a MBA and making six figures." Little did he know, my suit was from Macy's, my salary was in the low five figures and I only had a bachelors' degree. I laughed at his comment and wished him a good day. As I walked away I thought, "A stranger saw more in me than I saw in myself."

Mom's Messages

1. **God is constantly revealing truths to us, pay attention.**
2. **You will encounter some difficulties along the way; don't allow those difficulties to overwhelm you.**
3. **Enjoy the simple things in life.**

You Got To Be Kidding Me

**2 Corinthians 12:9 New International Version (NIV)
9 But he said to me, "My grace is sufficient for you, for my power is made perfect in weakness." Therefore I will boast all the more gladly about my weaknesses, so that Christ's power may rest on me.**

Motivation was relentless in her quest to cast me in bad light. Once during a weekly staff meeting, she announced a strange new departmental rule. She said "Effective immediately, everyone must notify Run-Tell-That when you leave the office for lunch." Run-Tell-That is Motivation's assistant. Translation, this rule only applies to Evolving but I have to say everyone for appearance sake. Immediately after hearing the announcement, I thought to myself "You got to be kidding me, we are professionals and we have to notify someone when we go to lunch."

It didn't take very long for suspicions to be put to rest. Per Motivation's instructions, I notified Run-Tell-That I was leaving for lunch. After lunch, I returned back to my desk and resumed working. Shortly after my return, Run-Tell-That appeared in the doorway of my office. She didn't beat around the bush, "You didn't let me know you were back from lunch." "Isn't it obvious, I replied?" "You are to notify me when you return from lunch." I replied, "That isn't what Motivation stated during the staff meeting, she told us to notify you when we leave not return. I suggest you guys put the rule in writing and I will post it on my bulletin board." Run-Tell-That became visibly aggravated with my response. "No one is going to put anything in writing for you, who do you think you are?" She turned away from me and headed to Motivation's office. I knew this spelled trouble for me but at this point I was not going to back down from Motivation.

A few minutes passed and then I heard it, a loud rumble barreling down the hall. It was Motivation and she was livid. "Why did you curse my assistant?" I turned away from my computer to acknowledge Motivation's presence. Motivation's voice apparently drew the attention of my fellow co-workers. I could hear their chairs rolling back from their desk and I could hear a couple of them say they were going to the break room. I replied, "I didn't curse Run-Tell-That, I simply told her she should put the new rule in writing." Motivation voice went up at least two octaves. I turned away and resumed working. "Do you hear me talking to you, Motivation stated?" I turned my attention towards Motivation. "I will not listen to you unless you lower your voice." Motivation paused for a moment as if she had to catch her breath then she responded: "You are not to speak to Run-Tell-That in a disrespectful manner." "Motivation you never asked me what was said, you simply took Run-Tell-That story and ran with it" I replied. Motivation starred at me and then stormed away. I got up from my desk as she left. As I watched her walk down to her office I laughed to myself. In that moment, Motivation reminded me of Ms. Sophia walking through the corn fields in "The Color Purple".

The next morning I arrived to the office around 7AM. I turned on my computer, and began to read and respond to e-mails. Motivation, her assistant and I are normally the first into work each morning. By the time I got to my desk the phone was ringing, it was Motivation. "MGH Evolving speaking, may I help you?" "This is Motivation I need to see you in my office now. Run-Tell-That and I want to discuss what happened on yesterday." I was between a rock and a hard place, I knew if I told Motivation I wasn't coming I would be written up for insubordination and if I met with her and Run-Tell-That alone it would be their words against mine. I had to think quickly so I responded. "I will meet with you but I am going to contact someone from human relations to attend the meeting." Motivation said that would be fine. I contacted the relations department, I told the representative the story and she scheduled a time to come up to speak with Run-Tell-That, Motivation and me.

The representative arrived later that afternoon. I was paged to Motivation's office. Motivation and the representative were already engaged in conversation. I spoke to both of the ladies and took a seat. I immediately noticed Run-Tell-That was conspicuously absent from the room. This struck me as strange because my

The Devil Goes To Work Too

conversation with Run-Tell-That was the primary reason Motivation called the meeting.

After I greeted the ladies, I told the Human Relations representative I requested her presence at the meeting because the Run-Tell-That and Motivation were accusing me of cursing Run-Tell-That when she questioned me about notifying her when I return from lunch. The HR representative listened intently to my comments. When I finished speaking, she turned her attention to Motivation. Motivation, can you tell me what problems are you having with Evolving? "He is creating a hostile work environment for me and the rest of his co-workers, everyone is afraid of him. For example: yesterday, Run-Tell-That went to his office to find out why he didn't notify her he had returned from lunch and he cursed her." I sat quietly waiting for my turn to speak, I was calm on the outside but I was fuming on the inside. I thought, how is this lady sitting here and lying with a straight face. After Motivation completed her statement, the representative turned in my direction. "Evolving, did you curse Run-Tell-That?" "No I did not. Run-Tell-That comes to my office and accused me of breaking a rule. I told her I didn't, she got mad made a statement and stormed away. Later Motivation accused me of saying ill things to Run-Tell-That." After I completed my statement, the HR representative asks Motivation "Why did Run-Tell-That engage in conversation with Evolving? It was obvious he was at his desk. Did you or Run-Tell-That need him to do something?" "No", Motivation replied. "In my opinion you guys are bothering Evolving. He was at his desk and performing his job", the rep. replied. Motivation my advice for you is to create a sign-in sheet for employees, this will alleviate the issue of trying to find out when someone leaves or returns from lunch."

From the look on Motivation's face, she was visibly shaken and apparently disappointed in the representative's recommendations. The HR person gave Motivation and I her card. "If you guys need me for anything, don't hesitate to call me." We both thanked the rep. for meeting with us. The representative shook both of our hands as she and I exited Motivation's office.

The rest of the day was eerily quiet. No one said anything to me and I didn't say anything to anyone. As I was leaving for the day, I noticed Run-Tell-That had created a sign-in sheet. While waiting on the elevator to come, I see Motivation through the glass door she is heading in my direction. It turns out she was leaving for the day as well. I thought, "this is going to be an awkward ride down." The elevator finally arrived. I held the door so Motivation could enter first. As the doors to the elevator closed, Motivation looks at me and says "You are nothing but a trouble maker." I respond to her, "God bless you." That day I learned how powerful the name of God is, all you have to do is call him and your enemy will retreat. Motivation didn't have anything to say after my comment. She stood silently in the corner looking up at the lights in the elevator. Before I knew it the doors to the elevator opened, we both proceeded to the parking deck.

Mom's Messages

1. **Don't set traps for folks. The trap you set could end up trapping you.**
2. **Be still, God will fight your battles.**
3. **Listen before you speak and God will provide you with an adequate response.**
4. **The way high is low.**

Give Praise

Saying thank you for a job well done, providing incentives for above average performance, throwing a celebration for continuous achievement, making smoothies, having junk days on Fridays are some of the ways I have shown appreciation to my employees over the years. Some of my colleagues have criticized me for giving my personal funds and setting aside time to recognize and reward persons for doing a job they are paid to do. I think taking the time to express your appreciation in tangible ways shows your employees you care about them on a personal level.

Some years ago I was in church and the pastor said something that has stayed with me until this day. The sermon was about being a representative of God. Towards the end of the sermon, he said: "It a poor frog that won't praise its own pond." In other words if you can't say something good about something you are a part of, what does that say about you?

Mom's Messages

1. **Do something nice, just because.**
2. **Be the first to point out the good you see in others.**

Thank You Lord

Proverbs 3:5-6 New International Version (NIV)
⁵ Trust in the Lord with all your heart and lean not on your own understanding; ⁶ in all your ways submit to him, and he will make your paths straight.[a]

One of the most difficult realities I had to face in my professional and personal life was accepting responsibility for my actions or inactions. I finally realized if my circumstance were going to change for the better my attitude regarding my circumstance would have to change. I had a habit of attributing my failures, miscues, disappointments in life to other people or outside influences. I had a difficult time coming to grips with the idea that I am where I am in life as a result of something I did or left undone.

Growing up there were three things that contributed to me not being able to excel: Today, I realize all I have achieved and every obstacle I have overcome is rooted in my belief that God is in control and if I allow him to lead me the victory would be mine and the glory would be his. There were four things I encountered in my life that kept me from trying: low expectations from others, fear of failure, fear of not being accepted and pride. The one thing that made me try was hope. My experience has taught me for he is my God and I am his servant.

Growing up in a low income, drug and crime infested neighborhood, receiving a less than adequate education and having parents of meager means; I was equipped with all the excuses I needed to justify my failures in life. While I never revealed my thoughts to anyone, these thoughts made me a captive of my own choosing. During my undergraduate years in college, I often told myself my bad grades on test or having to repeat a course was attributed to my background. I never considered my failures were due to the fact that I didn't study like I should have. I never considered the fact that I took poor notes or didn't take notes in class or rarely solicited help from my professors or fellow classmates, never participated in study groups and rarely opened my text books. Most often my preparation for an exam consisted of me staying up late and cramming the night before.

Upon graduating from college by the grace of God, I had a harsh reality to face. I had a college degree but my low GPA and lack of practical work experience made landing my first professional position a big challenge. After months of being unsuccessful in finding a job and having family and friends ask me what I was doing, I began to make excuses. My favorite one was: it's who you know not what you know. My family and friends in an attempt to offer support would agree. They would chime in and say, you are right. On occasion they would add additional excuses to the list.

After six months of pounding the payment and no job to show for it, my words were true but my logic was flawed. You can't have a better contact than God. He will work on you where you are and guide you to where he wants you to be. Making the vow to God was my first recollection of me taking responsibility for my own actions. I don't want anyone to think just because I changed my outlook that everything was easy for me, to the contrary I had even bigger challenges after that. I quickly learned everyone doesn't value hard work and everyone doesn't want you to succeed. Despite the actions of the enemy I was determined to keep moving forward.

Mom's Messages

1. **Do a self -analysis**
2. **You will not win every time**
3. **You will not be defeated every time**
4. **Face your fears (Stop settling for leftovers)**
5. **Your best efforts will yield your best results**
6. **Have faith and work towards a goal**

It Is What It Is...

Luke 6:37 New International Version (NIV)
37 "Do not judge, and you will not be judged. Do not condemn, and you will not be condemned. Forgive, and you will be forgiven.

Growing up I was taught to be nice, treat everybody with respect, and be fair in making decisions. For the most part, I have done a good job at that. I would learn later in life being kind and fair to people doesn't guarantee they will reciprocate the favor. Often times I have experienced work place situations that left me scratching my head. The following questions came to mind: Why did a person respond a certain way towards me? Why didn't some of my most thoroughly planned projects fail? Why do agendas set by people with evil intentions succeed? Why does God allow trials and tribulations in my life? My conclusion is quite elementary, things will happen to me for reasons unknown to me but I have the assurance it will all work out for my good. There is no clearer example of this than the experiences I had with two employees at Spirit Hospital.

Misery-Loves-Company and Throw-Stones-N-Hide-Her-Hands were members of my management team. I later learned these two ladies were the individuals who reported me to HR. I shared information regarding

The Devil Goes To Work Too

the compliance calls with them a few days before I was fired. One of the individuals, Throw-Stones-N-Hide-Her-Hands called me the evening I was fired. Hi Evolving, this is Throw-Stones-N-Hide-Her-Hands. "What happened?" "I was fired." I replied. "Really, I didn't know why the boss and the HR guy came over. I thought it was a good visit because I heard laughing." "No Throw-Stones-N-Hide-Her-Hands it wasn't a good visit." The next comment made by Throw-Stones-N-Hide-Her-Hands was really strange to me. Instead of her offering words of encouragement or comfort she said "It was fun." I replied, "Ok". An awkward silence followed my response. I thanked Throw-Stones for calling and said goodbye.

Throw-Stones-N-Hide-Her-Hands was an individual I approached with a high degree of caution. I quickly learned she wasn't a member of the Evolving fan club. Quite the opposite, Throw-Stones-N-Hide-Her-Hands had a tough time accepting me as her boss and it was obvious. She had worked for Spirit Hospital for over twenty-five years and resented administration for not considering her for my position. During my first three months at Spirit, Throw-Stones-N-Hide-Her-Hands continued to have meetings with outside vendors and made decisions without my involvement. Some employees informed me she told them I was just a consultant and wouldn't be there long. I tried to be understanding and patient with her. Initially I thought Throw-Stones-N-Hide-Her-Hands feelings towards me would change once she realized I was not a threat to her. Not the case at all, she would call around to my direct reports to inquire of my whereabouts. Often times while I was speaking to staff members at their desks, she would walk up to listen to the conversation.

Although the skepticism was there and there were some members of the management team I trusted more than others, I always made sure I shared information equally with the management team. I wanted to avoid the appearance of being biased to one person over the other.

A few days after Throw-Stones-N-Hide-Her-Hands phone call, the other individual whom I spoke with regarding the compliance call, Misery-Loves-Company called. "Hey Evolving, This is Misery-Loves-Company, I heard what happen, I wasn't even there. I was off for a funeral." "Sorry to hear that Misery-Loves-Company, are you and the family ok?" "We alright, how are you?" I replied, "It was really foul how they got rid of me, they never asked my side of the story." She replied, "Don't even worry about it, now you can write your book." I felt some kind of way about her comment so instead of saying something really mean I told her I was having lunch with a friend and had to end the call. "Ok I will talk to you later Evolving." "Goodbye Misery." A month later Misery-Loves-Company called me again to inform me that Ms. Nice-Nasty, a member of the management team was promoted to Director. "Hello." Hey Evolving, this is Misery-Loves-Company. Did your fake friend

The Devil Goes To Work Too

call you to tell you she got promoted?" "Who are you referring to Misery-Loves-Company?" "You know that evil manager, Nice-Nasty. Throw-Stones-N-Hide-Her-Hands and I were having a conversation the other day about how things went down in your situation and we think she was the one who got you fired." "I don't believe that Misery-Loves-Company, she may have her ways but I don't see her doing something like that." Misery-Loves-Company replied, "Whatever, you better wake up. Have you talked to her since you been gone?" I saw Misery-Loves-Company was trying to make me angry with Nice-Nasty. I think she believed I would give her information if I thought Nice-Nasty turned me into HR. "I have only spoken to her once Misery-Loves-Company. Someone is buzzing in on the other line, I will talk to you later." "Ok, bye" Misery-Loves-Company replied. "Goodbye."

Prior to my arriving at Spirit Hospital, I was warned to stay away from Misery-Loves-Company. Here reputation preceded her. I was told she was mean and bitter. A few months earlier, Misery-Loves-Company was demoted to another role within the department. Instead of me heeding that advice, I was determined I would be the one to bring out the good in her. Wrong, I now realize the good in her was buried so deep beneath pain of her personal and work life disappointments she had forgotten what good felt like so she could not share good feelings for others. The only emotion Misery-Loves-Company was capable of sharing was misery.

Her goal was to make everyone she came in contact with feel all the bad things she had experienced in life. Little did she know the joy I had wasn't given by her so she didn't have the power to take it away.

Months after being fired from Spirit, God opened up a new and greater work opportunity for me and like Misery-Loves-Company said I had an opportunity to write my book. To God, glory forever and ever. Amen.

Mom's Messages

1. **Don't fret over the attacks of your enemies, you win in the end.**
2. **Be motivated by your convictions, not revenge. One path leads to self-awareness the other leads to self-defeat.**
3. **Fill your jar with joy not jelly beans.**
4. **If a person reveals their true self to you, believe them and respond accordingly.**

References

Holy Bible, New International Version®, NIV®
Copyright ©1973, 1978, 1984, 2011 by Biblica, Inc.®
Used by permission. All rights reserved worldwide.

New American Standard Bible (NASB)
Copyright © 1960, 1962, 1963, 1968, 1971, 1972,
1973, 1975, 1977, 1995 by The Lockman Foundation

About the Author

Carlos Taylor was born and raised in Birmingham, AL. Carlos finds strength in his love of God and is surrounded by the love and support of his family and friends. Being one of five siblings, Carlos identified his strength of inspiring others very early in in life. Carlos earned both his Bachelors of Science and Masters of Health Administration from the University of Alabama Birmingham. Carlos currently works in the healthcare industry as a Client Delivery Director.

Carlos credits his success to the love, support and encouragement from his parents who instilled in him that he can accomplish any goals he set for himself through hard work, determination and by always keeping God first. Throughout his career, Carlos has successfully managed over ninety employees. He credits his success as a leader to respecting, inspiring, and encouraging his employees to be the best person they can be at work and in their personal lives.

Carlos enjoys his work and considers each day a new learning experience, a source of his writing. He finds great joy in sharing through his writing to encourage and uplift others no matter what obstacles they may face at work.